51 ESSENTIAL AI TERMS EXPLAINED FOR LEADERS

A Non-Technical Guide. Each Term Defined, Explained And With A Practical Example To Increase Your Leadership Impact

MARCO RYAN

CONTENTS

INTRODUCTION

In the heart of Kenya's savanna, a small not-for-profit organization fully captures how AI and human collaboration can drive transformative change. Here, amid the vast expanse of acacia-dotted landscapes, an unlikely alliance between artificial intelligence and dedicated conservationists is rewriting the future of wildlife conservation. The Mara Elephant Project is a pioneering initiative dedicated to protecting the region's majestic elephants, which poachers and human-wildlife conflict constantly threaten.

The project harnesses an innovative tracking system that analyzes elephant movement patterns across the Maasai Mara. Once indecipherable "noise," these patterns are now intricately mapped with precision, predicting potential human-elephant conflicts before they occur. The system, powered by AI algorithms, processes real-time data from GPS trackers fitted on elephants, alerting rangers to unusual movements that could indicate poachers' presence or potential entry into farmlands.

This cutting-edge approach transforms traditional conservation tactics, enabling preemptive action to protect elephants and local communities. Rangers, once reliant on delayed reports and sporadic sightings, now operate with a newfound efficiency guided by the foresight AI provides. This collaboration extends beyond just tracking; it involves using drone technology to deter elephants gently from straying into agricultural lands, thus preventing the age-old conflict between humans and wildlife.

This project's success is a testament to the power of human ingenuity augmented by AI. It showcases a future where technology is not a distant, cold entity but a vital ally in solving some of the world's most pressing challenges. In the vastness of the Kenyan savanna, AI and humans work hand in hand, forging a new path for conservation.

This story is a compelling example of AI's potential for good. It illustrates how technology, when guided by human compassion and understanding, can create solutions that protect our planet's precious wildlife and ecosystems. It's a vivid reminder that the future of AI is not just about machines and algorithms but about the harmonious coexistence of human creativity and technological advancement.

In a world where artificial intelligence (AI) is no longer the province of speculative fiction but a stark reality shaping the present and future of business, understanding AI becomes imperative for leaders, whether CEOs or Kenyan Park Rangers.

The book "51 Essential AI Terms Explained for Leaders" emerges as a vital resource in this context. Tailored for time-poor business leaders yet driven by a relentless quest for excellence, this book aims to transform confusion into clarity, curiosity, and command over AI's potential. The narrative begins with an exploration of AI's transformative power, demonstrated through a series of strategically selected terms that encapsulate artificial intelligence's essence and expansive impact in the modern business arena.

USING THE BOOK

Structured to serve as both a primer and a reference, the book's layout is intuitive by design. Terms are arranged alphabetically, ensuring that you can quickly find definitions, explanations, and practical examples that bring to life, in simple, straight-forward terms, the relevance to your role as a leader. Whether in the midst of a high-stakes meeting or strategizing for your company's future, this book stands ready as your indispensable guide to navigating the AI landscape.

Beyond the definitions, each term is accompanied by a jargon-free explanation grounded in real-world applications to provide understanding and actionable in-sights. These explanations bridge the gap between theoretical AI constructs and their practical implications for your business, spotlighting AI's potential to drive innovation, efficiency, and competitive advantage.

Moreover, the book is punctuated with mini-case studies illustrating successful AI adoption, integration, and deployment across various industries. These examples offer a glimpse into how other leaders have harnessed AI to solve complex prob-ems, optimize operations, and carve out new market opportunities. They are not only instructive but also inspirational, showcasing the art of the possible in the realm of AI.

INCREASING YOUR IMPACT

The journey through the world of AI is one of continuous learning and adaptation. "51 Essential AI Terms Explained for Leaders" is not merely a compendium of terms but hopefully a practical and reliable guide steering you towards increased impact in your leadership role. By demystifying AI, the book empowers you to engage with technology not as a distant observer but as an informed, confident participant in the ongoing digital transformation.

This book also touches on the critical areas of AI ethics and regulation, equipping you with the knowledge to navigate the complex moral and legal landscape surrounding AI. Understanding these aspects is paramount for leaders committed to responsible AI implementation, ensuring innovation is pursued without compromising ethical standards or societal values.

As part of the "Leadership Impact Series," this volume underscores the series' commitment to enhancing leadership capabilities in technical domains. The journey toward mastering AI is akin to embarking on a path of continuous growth, where each step forward amplifies your ability to lead with vision, insight, and integrity in an increasingly digital world.

The book culminates with a call to action, urging you to leverage the knowledge gained to drive tangible change within your organization and industry. By embracing AI, you position your business for future success and contribute to shaping a future where technology amplifies human potential rather than supplanting it.

In crafting this guide, we draw upon extensive experience in AI and strive to distill complex concepts into accessible, actionable knowledge. Our goal is to equip you with the tools necessary to confidently navigate the AI landscape and foster a culture of innovation and forward-thinking within your organization.

As you delve into the book, approach each term with curiosity and an open mind, considering how the concepts presented can be applied to your unique challenges and opportunities. Remember, the field of AI is dynamic, continually evolving in response to discoveries, technologies, and societal needs. Similarly, your journey with AI should be one of perpetual exploration, learning, and adaptation.

We invite you to use this book not just as a resource but as a catalyst for broader engagement with AI. It will inspire you to explore further, question deeper, and innovate smarter. In doing so, you will enhance your own leadership impact and con-tribute to driving meaningful progress in your organization and the wider world.

The path to leadership excellence in the age of AI begins with understanding its language and potential. With "51 Essential AI Terms Explained for Leaders," that path is demystified, inviting you to step forward with the knowledge and confidence to embrace the transformative power of artificial intelligence.

Let this journey be both enlightening and empowering as we navigate the exciting landscape of AI together, shaping a future where technology and human ingenuity converge to create unprecedented opportunities for growth, innovation, and impact.

Chapter One

FROM A TO B

ALGORITHM

DEFINITION

A set of rules or instructions designed to perform a specific task or solve a problem.

ALGORITHM EXPLAINED

Imagine you have a recipe for your favorite dish. This recipe, with its step-by-step instructions on mixing and cooking ingredients, is similar to an algorithm. In Artificial Intelligence (AI), algorithms are like these recipes but for computers. They tell the computer how to process information, make decisions, and solve problems. From playing chess to recommending what movie you should watch next, algorithms power the brains behind AI systems, making them smart and responsive.

AN ALGORITHM EXAMPLE

Spotify – the music streaming service – has been one of the earliest exponents of AI. Their algorithms act like finely tuned curators and experts seeking to optimize personalized music recommendations for each user. That personalization journey begins with a simple interaction: a play, a pause, or a skip on any given track. Even just stopping after a few seconds of listening to a track tells Spotify something about you and your listening habits. Whether you browse by artists and albums or look for other playlists, every interaction with Spotify is recorded to fine-tune the recommendations and personalization engine that is the hallmark of their success.

Let's take the hypothetical example of Alex, a jazz enthusiast with a penchant for discovering underground artists. Like diligent anthropologists, Spotify's algorithms analyze all the nuances of Alex's musical tastes, mapping out a vast network of related artists and genres. This is not merely a technical process but a bespoke use of data, where each click or interaction creates a unique pathway and profile. That can be stored, referenced, and compared to similar nuanced profiles for other "Alexs."

The result for Alex is a playlist, seemingly handcrafted, filled with gems from familiar and obscure corners of the jazz world. It's a journey that starts in the smoky jazz clubs of New Orleans and traverses through the vibrant streets of Harlem, with each song telling a part of Alex's musical story. This personal touch, facilitated by the invisible hand of algorithms, transforms Spotify from a mere service to a companion in Alex's musical exploration.

ARTIFICIAL INTELLIGENCE (AI)

DEFINITION

Artificial intelligence is technology that enables computers to solve problems by simulating human intelligence and to mimic their actions.

ARTIFICIAL INTELLIGENCE EXPLAINED

AI is a broad field of computer science focused on creating smart machines capable of performing tasks that typically require human intelligence. These tasks include learning from experiences, understanding language, recognizing patterns, and making decisions. Imagine a robot that can converse with you, understand your questions, and provide answers like a human would. That's AI in action. AI is not just about robots, though; it also powers the voice assistant on your phone, predicts the weather, and even helps doctors diagnose diseases more accurately.

AN ARTIFICIAL INTELLIGENCE EXAMPLE

IBM's Watson, a computing system capable of understanding natural language, burst into the public consciousness in 2011, not through a scientific journal or a tech conference, but by competing on the quiz show "Jeopardy!" Against two of the show's greatest champions, Watson was not just a participant but a formidable contender, showcasing the power of AI to a broad audience.

Watson's journey began long before its television debut, rooted in IBM's dedication to advancing natural language processing. Its triumph on "Jeopardy!" was a watershed

3

moment, demonstrating AI's ability to digest and analyze vast amounts of information more quickly and accurately than ever before. But the story didn't end there; it was merely the prologue.

Post-victory, Watson's capabilities were channeled into more profound endeavors. One of the most impactful is its application in healthcare, specifically in oncology. Here, Watson assists physicians by sifting through millions of medical documents, research papers, and patient records to suggest personalized treatment options for cancer patients. This transition from a game show contestant to a medical assistant underscores a pivotal shift in AI's narrative: from demonstrating potential to making tangible impacts on human lives.

Through collaborations with healthcare institutions, Watson is part of a larger narrative in which AI becomes a beacon of hope for patients and a tool for physicians to combat one of humanity's most daunting challenges. IBM's releases and healthcare studies extensively document this story of evolution from entertainment to life-saving technology, painting a picture of an AI system that continues to learn, adapt, and serve humanity.

AUGMENTED INTELLIGENCE

DEFINITION

Augmented intelligence refers to the enhancement of human intelligence through technology. It emphasizes artificial intelligence's assistive role, working alongside humans to enhance cognitive performance rather than replacing it.

AUGMENTED INTELLIGENCE EXPLAINED

Augmented intelligence combines AI's processing power with human judgment and creativity. It's used in various fields to improve decision-making, productivity, and innovation by providing humans with enhanced capabilities through AI support.

AN AUGMENTED INTELLIGENCE EXAMPLE

In the financial sector, JP Morgan Chase's Contract Intelligence (COiN) platform exemplifies augmented intelligence by automating the interpretation of commercial loan agreements. Traditionally, legal staff required approximately 360,000 hours of work annually to perform this labor-intensive task. With COiN, the process is reduced to seconds, significantly improving efficiency and accuracy.

The platform's ability to quickly analyze and extract critical data from documents speeds up operations and allows employees to focus on more strategic tasks, enhancing overall productivity. This case, discussed in "Forbes" and other business publications, highlights how augmented intelligence can transform industries by automating complex, time-consuming processes while enhancing human capabilities.

AUTONOMOUS VEHICLES

DEFINITION

Vehicles that are capable of sensing their environment and navigating without human input.

AUTONOMOUS VEHICLES EXPLAINED

Autonomous vehicles, or self-driving cars, use a combination of sensors, cameras, radar, and artificial intelligence to travel from one place to another without needing a human driver. These vehicles can detect surroundings, make decisions, and navigate roads, traffic, and obstacles with remarkable accuracy and safety.

AN AUTONOMOUS VEHICLE EXAMPLE

Waymo, a pioneer in autonomous driving technology, embarked on an ambitious journey to transform transportation through self-driving vehicles. In a groundbreaking project in Phoenix, Arizona, Waymo launched a fully autonomous ride-hailing service, allowing residents to experience the future of urban mobility firsthand.

This service, detailed in transportation and technology media, offers a glimpse into a world where commutes are safer, more efficient, and accessible. Users recount the surreal experience of entering a vehicle without a driver, marveling at the car's ability to navigate complex urban environments easily. One notable journey involved a Waymo vehicle expertly handling a sudden road closure due to construction, rerouting in real-time without human intervention.

These stories from Phoenix residents highlight the technological marvels behind autonomous vehicles and their potential to redefine our relationship with transportation. They promise a future where road accidents decrease, traffic flows more smoothly, and the barriers to mobility for those unable to drive are removed.

BIG DATA

DEFINITION

"Big Data" refers to extremely large sets of information that are too complex, large, or fast-moving for traditional data processing software to manage and process.

BIG DATA EXPLAINED

What marks "Big Data" out from normal data is characterized by the three Vs: Volume, Velocity, and Variety. "Volume" refers to the amount of data gathered from various sources, including social media, business transactions, online interactions, and sensors. "Velocity" is the speed at which that data can be sourced or added to – usually measured in fractions of a second, depending on the sensor or source. Lastly, "Variety" refers to the different formats of data that can be sourced and stored together, such as structured data (in databases), unstructured data (text, images, video), and semi-structured data (XML files). It is the fusion of these three "Vs." that gives Big Data its unique characteristics and that, when analyzed, can uncover insights into previously invisible consumer behavior, economic trends, and other patterns, helping organizations make more informed decisions.

A BIG DATA EXAMPLE

Netflix's success story with big data analytics illustrates its power in content personalization and recommendation. By analyzing data from millions of subscribers, including their viewing habits, search history, and ratings, Netflix tailors its content and recommendations to individual tastes.

An example that stands out is the creation and success of the series "House of Cards." Netflix's big data analysis revealed a significant overlap in users who enjoyed political dramas, Kevin Spacey films, and the work of director David Fincher. Leveraging this insight, Netflix produced "House of Cards" and tailored its marketing strategies to target this specific audience intersection. This resulted in a hit show that increased subscription numbers and viewer engagement.

Chapter Two

JUST THE LETTER C

CHATBOT

Definition

A computer program designed to simulate conversation with human users, especially over the Internet.

CHATBOT EXPLAINED

Chatbots are like virtual assistants that can chat with you. They are programmed to understand questions or commands and provide responses or perform tasks accordingly. You might have encountered chatbots on websites as customer service agents that pop up to offer help. These chatbots can answer your questions, guide you through a website, or even assist with purchases, all without a human on the other side of the conversation. They're designed to make getting information and completing tasks easier and faster and are available 24/7.

A CHATBOT EXAMPLE

In fast food, Domino's Pizza introduced an innovative way to order a pizza through a chatbot named "Dom." This virtual chef, however, is not just a gimmick but a reflection of the changing landscape of customer service and engagement.

The story of Dom begins with the challenge of making ordering pizza as effortless as possible; in an era where speed and convenience reign supreme, Domino's recognized the need to engage with customers where they spend a significant portion of their time: on social media platforms. Thus, Dom was born not in a kitchen but within software engineers' intricate coding, aiming to bridge the gap between craving and satisfaction.

Imagine a late-night study session where a group of college students decides to order pizza. Instead of navigating through apps or websites, they message Dom on Facebook Messenger. Through natural language processing, Dom understands their order, confirms the details, and even cracks a joke or two, adding a layer of personality to the transaction. This convenience and engagement are not accidental but result from careful design and understanding of customer behavior.

CLOUD COMPUTING

DEFINITION

Cloud computing is the delivery of computing services—servers, storage, databases, networking, software—over the Internet, offering faster innovation, flexible resources, and economies of scale.

CLOUD COMPUTING EXPLAINED

Cloud computing revolutionizes how businesses operate by allowing them to access and manage vast computing resources over the Internet without investing in and maintaining physical servers and data centers. This approach will enable businesses to scale services up or down based on demand, ensuring they only pay for what they use. It also facilitates innovation by providing access to the latest technologies. Moreover, cloud services can be accessed from anywhere, promoting collaboration among teams regardless of location. For businesses, this means improved efficiency, cost savings, and the ability to adapt to market changes quickly.

A CLOUD COMPUTING EXAMPLE

In an era where digital transformation shapes the direction of humanitarian efforts, the International Federation of Red Cross and Red Crescent Societies (IFRC) has been harnessing the power of cloud computing to enhance its mission of saving lives and fostering resilience in communities around the globe.

The IFRC's strategic partnership with leading cloud service providers is at the heart of this transformation. The organization can collect, process, and analyze real-time data from disaster zones using cloud-based platforms. This data-driven approach enables the IFRC to make informed decisions, optimize resource allocation, and coordinate more effectively with local authorities and partner organizations. Moreover, cloud technologies facilitate the secure storage and sharing of critical information, enhancing collaboration across the global Red Cross and Red Crescent network.

Furthermore, cloud computing supports the IFRC's commitment to innovation and continuous learning. Through online training platforms hosted in the cloud, volunteers and staff worldwide access essential training materials, ensuring they are equipped with the latest knowledge and skills to respond to crises effectively.

COGNITIVE COMPUTING

DEFINITION

A subset of AI that attempts to mimic human thought processes in a computerized model.

COGNITIVE COMPUTING EXPLAINED

Cognitive computing systems are designed to learn and interact naturally with humans, aiming to simulate human thought processes in a complex manner. These systems use self-learning algorithms that incorporate data mining, pattern recognition, and natural language processing to mimic the human brain. They intend to help decision-making by analyzing large amounts of data with a human-like understanding.

A COGNITIVE COMPUTING EXAMPLE

In the vibrant city of Barcelona, a remarkable transformation unfolded as it embarked on a mission to redefine itself as a smart city leader, steering clear of the paths trodden by giants like IBM. At the core of this transformation was the integration of a pioneering cognitive computing system designed to weave through the city's complex urban fabric and enhance the lives of its residents.

This advanced system, a collaboration between Barcelona and a consortium of tech firms, digested vast data streams from IoT devices, sensors, and social media, mirroring human thought processes to provide insights that shaped smarter city living. It revolutionized waste management by predicting waste generation patterns, leading to optimized collection routes that cut costs and environmental footprint. Public safety saw a new dawn as the system analyzed real-time data from surveillance cameras and emergency calls, deploying police and emergency services swiftly to where they were needed most.

Barcelona's journey into cognitive computing showcases a future where technology empowers urban spaces to be more responsive, sustainable, and safe. It's a testament to the city's innovative spirit, proving how cognitive computing can solve complex urban challenges and make cities smarter, more humane, and livable.

CONVERSATIONAL AI

DEFINITION

Conversational AI refers to artificial intelligence technologies, like chatbots or virtual assistants, that can engage in human-like dialogue, understand natural language, and respond in a way that mimics human conversation.

CONVERSATIONAL AI EXPLAINED

It powers various applications, from website customer service bots to voice-activated smartphone assistants. Conversational AI interprets and processes users' requests through natural language processing and machine learning, providing personalized, interactive communication experiences.

A CONVERSATIONAL AI EXAMPLE

"Bank of America" introduced Erica, a conversational AI assistant who provides 24/7 customer support and handles inquiries ranging from account balances to transaction disputes. Unlike traditional chatbots, this AI assistant can contextually understand customer requests, remember past interactions, and even handle multi-turn conversations, offering solutions and guidance in real-time.

Within months of deployment, the bank reported a significant increase in customer satisfaction scores and a reduction in live agent call volumes. Customers appreciated the instant, round-the-clock support, which highlighted the AI assistant's ability to efficiently resolve complex queries. This implementation, spotlighted in financial technology reviews, demonstrates conversational AI's capacity to transform customer service and offers insights into future banking experiences that prioritize accessibility, personalization, and efficiency.

CONVOLUTIONAL NEURAL NETWORKS (CNN)

DEFINITION

A class of deep neural networks most commonly applied to analyzing visual imagery.

CNN EXPLAINED

CNNs are built to understand and organize information from images, like how our eyes and brains see and recognize different objects, shapes, and textures. They're like smart learners who can pick up on patterns and details in pictures without being told what to look for. This makes them incredibly useful for recognizing and sorting images and videos, figuring out what's in them, or even analyzing medical pictures to help doctors.

A CNN EXAMPLE

In the quiet corridors of Moorfields Eye Hospital in London, an unusual collaboration between medical professionals and artificial intelligence (AI) experts has unveiled the potential of Convolutional Neural Networks (CNNs) to revolutionize the field of ophthalmology. The project, a partnership with DeepMind Technologies, aimed to harness the power of CNNs to analyze eye scans with unprecedented accuracy.

The CNN system developed for Moorfields was trained on thousands of anonymized eye scans, learning to detect and diagnose more than 50 types of eye conditions as accurately as the world's leading ophthalmologists. This AI-driven approach promises to expedite the diagnosis process and significantly enhance the precision of detecting ailments that could lead to blindness, such as glaucoma and age-related macular degeneration.

By learning from vast datasets of eye scans, the CNN model mimics the intricate process of human visual recognition, offering a faster, more accurate diagnostic tool. This innovation paves the way for early and more efficient treatment of eye conditions. It exemplifies the broader potential of AI to augment and enhance medical diagnostics, profoundly impacting patient care and outcomes.

Chapter Three
FROM D TO E

DATA MINING

DEFINITION

The process of discovering patterns and knowledge from large amounts of data. The data sources include databases, data warehouses, the Internet, and others.

DATA MINING EXPLAINED

Data mining is like digging through a massive pile of information to find valuable nuggets of knowledge. Think of it as a treasure hunt, where the treasure is insights into what customers like, what products could be best sellers, or how to keep customers coming back. Using special tools and formulas, businesses can sift through all their data to spot significant trends and patterns they didn't see before. It can be used for various purposes, including market research, product development, and customer retention. By applying algorithms to data, businesses can uncover hidden patterns that help them make strategic decisions.

A DATA MINING EXAMPLE

Target, the retail giant, utilized data mining techniques to predict customer behavior and improve its marketing strategies. By analyzing purchase history data, Target identified patterns that indicated significant life events, such as pregnancies, among its customers. It ingeniously predicted a customer's pregnancy based on her shopping habits, even before the news was made public. This was achieved by identifying specific buying patterns and product preferences that tend to change as a customer enters different life stages. With this insight, Target could send tailored offers and coupons for baby-related products, significantly enhancing customer loyalty and sales in their baby product segment.

DECISION TREES

DEFINITION

A decision support tool that uses a tree-like graph or model of decisions and their possible consequences, including chance event outcomes, resource costs, and utility.

DECISION TREES EXPLAINED

Imagine you're in a maze with many turns; you must decide which way to go at each junction. A decision tree is like a map of that maze, laid out in a tree shape with branches representing all possible paths you can take. At every fork in the branches, a question helps you decide which way to go next, leading you closer to the exit or, in business terms, the best decision. In the digital realm, decision trees help computers learn from the past, asking simple questions to sort and understand new data, like separating apples from oranges. They turn intricate decisions into a series of straightforward steps, providing a clear path to the best choice.

A DECISION TREES EXAMPLE

In the sun-drenched vineyards of California's Napa Valley, a mid-sized winery has quietly been making waves for its robust Zinfandels and its innovative use of decision trees to uncork the complexities of wine production and sales strategies.

Faced with a saturated market and intricate production variables, the winery turned to decision trees to better predict which blends would satisfy its customer base's palate. The decision trees branched into patterns by analyzing historical sales data, customer preferences, and harvest yields, revealing which grapes to prioritize and how to blend them to appeal to different market segments.

The winery also applied decision trees in its marketing, identifying which customer demographics were likely to purchase high-end reserves versus those who preferred the more affordable table wines. This strategic approach resulted in targeted marketing campaigns, with tailored messaging and promotions that led to a marked increase in sales and customer retention.

DEEP LEARNING

DEFINITION

A subset of machine learning that uses neural networks with many layers to learn from vast amounts of data, enabling computers to identify patterns and make decisions with minimal human intervention.

DEEP LEARNING EXPLAINED

Deep learning is like teaching computers to mimic the human brain's learning process. Picture a young child gradually recognizing different fruit types by looking at them repeatedly. Similarly, deep learning allows a computer to learn how to perform tasks like recognizing speech or identifying images. It does this through layered networks—think of these as building blocks of knowledge, where each layer helps the computer filter information and focus on the details that matter. The more layers there are, the more refined the computer's learning and understanding becomes. This technology powers the face recognition on your phone and the voice assistant that plays your favorite song—examples of how deep learning is becoming an invisible but significant part of our daily lives.

A DEEP LEARNING EXAMPLE

In the bustling heart of New York City's healthcare system, Mount Sinai Hospital embraced a profound technological shift that brought deep learning prowess into medicine. This shift was personified by an algorithm named "Deep Patient."

Developed by the hospital's AI researchers, Deep Patient was fed an extensive array of health records from more than

700,000 individuals, learning to predict disease by discerning intricate patterns in the data that even experienced doctors might miss. When a new patient's information is entered, Deep Patient analyzes their medical history with the insight gleaned from this vast dataset.

One striking success story emerged when Deep Patient accurately predicted a patient's onset of schizophrenia. This feat had traditionally been challenging due to the disorder's complex nature and the subtlety of its early signs. For clinicians, this predictive power is a beacon of hope for early intervention strategies.

EDGE COMPUTING

DEFINITION

Edge computing processes data near or at the source of data generation rather than in a centralized data-processing warehouse.

EDGE COMPUTING EXPLAINED

Imagine you're at a crowded concert and trying to send a selfie to your friend. It could take a while if your phone signal has to travel far to a distant server and back. That's where edge computing comes in—it's like having a mini-server right at the concert, so your selfie gets to your friend super fast, without any annoying delay.

This concept is convenient for all our smart gadgets, from fitness trackers to smart fridges. These devices constantly gather data—like your steps or the temperature of your leftovers—and they often need to respond instantly. With edge computing, they can process this information on the spot. This approach is particularly beneficial for IoT devices and applications that require real-time processing and analysis, reducing latency and enhancing performance.

AN EDGE COMPUTING EXAMPLE

In the northern expanse of Norway, a small town's fisheries are riding the wave of digital transformation with edge computing at the helm. The city, known for its rich marine life, has outfitted its fishing fleet with sensors and edge computing devices that process data directly on the ships.

Previously, Nordkapp's vessels would collect oceanographic data during their voyages, which then required transmission to distant servers for analysis, a process marred by latency and connectivity issues inherent in the remote, bandwidth-starved Arctic Circle. However, with edge computing, data such as water temperature, fish populations, and equipment status are now analyzed locally in real-time. The result? Immediate insights lead to more strategic decisions on where to cast nets, optimal navigation routes, and proactive maintenance of on-board equipment.

The introduction of edge computing has conserved bandwidth and reduced delays, leading to more sustainable fishing practices by enabling the detection of optimal fishing areas, thus protecting against overfishing.

EVOLUTIONARY ALGORITHM

DEFINITION

A subset of artificial intelligence that solves problems using mechanisms inspired by biological evolution, such as reproduction, mutation, recombination, and selection.

EVOLUTIONARY ALGORITHMS EXPLAINED

Evolutionary algorithms are a fascinating blend of nature's principles and cutting-edge technology. Inspired by Darwin's theory of natural selection, these algorithms operate on the survival of the fittest. Imagine a group of robots solving a maze: over time, only the quickest, most efficient robots make it through. These top performers are then used to create a new generation of robots, inheriting the successful traits of their predecessors but with added tweaks for even better performance. This process repeats, constantly evolving and adapting, finding solutions to complex problems that mimic living organisms' evolutionary steps. From optimizing delivery routes to designing more efficient engines, evolutionary algorithms tackle challenges that stump traditional problem-solving methods, offering a glimpse into how the natural world can inspire technological innovation.

AN EVOLUTIONARY ALGORITHM EXAMPLE

The sweeping plains of Oklahoma are an unlikely setting for cutting-edge use of technology against nature, where the wind is both the narrative's leading character and the catalyst. However, an energy company has started using evolutionary algorithms to create the optimal wind farm design.

Wind farms, the company's knights in the battle against climate change, faced a challenge: how to place their turbines to capture the roaring winds without stepping on each other's toes—or blades, rather. The company turned to Darwin's evolutionary theory, which was encoded into an evolutionary algorithm that mimicked the survival of the fittest.

The digital model of the Oklahoma plains saw virtual turbines compete on a simulated field, with the algorithm selecting the most efficient layouts generation after generation. The fittest weren't the strongest or the fastest, but the smartest at catching the wind's breath.

Iterating through hundreds of digital generations, this process sculpted a wind farm that was both a monument to efficiency and a testament to the land's natural rhythms. The result was a dance of technology with the elements, producing more power with fewer turbines and less land and a gentle, rather than forceful, imprint upon the earth.

EXPLAINABLE AI (XAI)

DEFINITION

XAI is a set of processes and methods that allows human users to comprehend and trust the results and output created by machine learning algorithms. It seeks to address how AI systems make black-box decisions.

XAI EXPLAINED

Explainable AI is about making AI's decision-making process transparent and understandable to humans. This is crucial in sensitive and critical applications such as healthcare, finance, and legal decisions, where understanding the rationale behind AI's decisions is essential for trust and accountability.

AN XAI EXAMPLE

In the labyrinth of finance, where numbers and complex models dictate the ebb and flow of markets, a fintech startup named FinVisor has embarked on a journey to demystify the black box of algorithmic decision-making with the use of Explainable AI (XAI).

What began as a challenge for FinVisor - how to build trust with their customers when the very algorithms meant to guide them seemed inscrutable, even arcane – quickly became a differentiator. FinVisor's solution didn't lie in discarding the complex AI models that could predict market trends with astonishing accuracy but in making the AI's decisions understandable to the layperson.

FinVisor used XAI to create a system that accompanied every investment suggestion with a clear explanation. For instance, when the AI recommended a particular stock, it didn't just deliver a command; it provided a story—market trends, news sentiment, and performance metrics were woven into a narrative that clients could understand.

This approach turned the once opaque advice into transparent guidance. Clients of FinVisor could now see the 'why' behind the 'what,' which not only built confidence in the AI's recommendations but also empowered them with knowledge. As trust in the system grew, so did FinVisor's reputation, establishing them as pioneers in a new frontier where AI becomes less of a mysterious oracle and more of a trusted advisor.

Chapter Four
FROM F TO G

FACIAL RECOGNITION

DEFINITION

Facial recognition is a technology that identifies and verifies individuals by analyzing facial features through digital images or video frames.

FACIAL RECOGNITION EXPLAINED

Facial recognition is like a high-tech game of "Who's Who?" where a computer system plays detective, sifting through a crowd to find a match for a particular face. It analyzes specific features—think of them as facial landmarks—like the distance between the eyes or the shape of the jawline. This is similar to how you might recognize a friend in a sea of strangers by their unique features.

This technology is woven into our daily lives; it helps you unlock your phone just by looking at it and keeps public spaces secure by quickly spotting persons of interest. Its ability to swiftly identify has made it indispensable, offering convenience and enhancing safety. Whether it's keeping tabs on school attendance, helping shops personalize your shopping experience, or reuniting lost children with their families, facial recognition is a silent guardian and a subtle facilitator in our increasingly connected world.

A FACIAL RECOGNITION EXAMPLE

As dawn breaks over Hartsfield-Jackson Atlanta International Airport, the hustle of travelers is matched by the silent, watchful eyes of facial recognition technology. Delta Air Lines has turned to this sophisticated tech to rewrite the travel story from weary waits to excitement and opportunity.

Imagine a world where your face is not just a passport to emotions but also a destination. Delta's passengers step up to the kiosks where a quick photo is snapped, their identity is confirmed, and they're whisked away to their waiting planes. Documents remain tucked away as faces unlock the path ahead.

This isn't just about speed; it's about security woven seamlessly into travel. Delta's digital system cross-references faces with databases at lightning speed, ensuring that the person boarding the plane is the exact match to the ticket in hand.

But Delta's tale is noteworthy for more than streamlined boarding or bolstered security. It's the vision of a future where travel friction smooths into something more fluid—a journey where looking into a camera can mean leaping continents. This vision, featured in Delta's press releases and echoed in traveler testimonials, casts facial recognition not as a tool of high-tech surveillance but as a key to a more personalized, frictionless travel experience.

FEDERATED LEARNING

DEFINITION

Federated learning is a machine learning approach that trains an algorithm across multiple servers or other federated devices. Each holds local data samples without exchanging them. This method enables multiple participants to construct a common, robust machine learning model without sharing data, thus addressing privacy, security, and data access challenges.

FEDERATED LEARNING EXPLAINED

Federated learning is like a group project where instead of everyone gathering in one room to work together, each person does their part at home and then shares the results. In this tech-savvy group project, smartphones and devices learn tasks without sending data to a central server. They practice independently, learning to recognize your voice or predict text when you type. Then, these devices send their new knowledge—not the data they learned from—back to the central system. This method keeps your data private while helping the overall network get smarter. It's collaborative learning at its finest, with the bonus of securing personal information. This could mean more personalized apps and services without exposing your personal data.

A FEDERATED LEARNING EXAMPLE

In the sprawling city of Toronto, a financial tech startup called "SecureSpends" is rewriting the rules of data privacy and machine learning with federated learning. Amid rising concerns over data misuse, SecureSpends offers a breath of fresh air: a privacy-centric way to make its fraud detection systems more intelligent without compromising sensitive information.

Thousands of transactions occur across the city each day. SecureSpends' technology lives in the smartphones in people's pockets, learning to spot signs of fraudulent activity on each device individually. Instead of sending customers' financial information back to a central server, the devices are trained locally and only share their insights—the learnings, not the data itself.

The result? A constantly evolving collective intelligence. Every phone acts like a neuron in a vast brain, contributing to a smarter, more secure system. SecureSpends' breakthrough showcases a future where privacy and smart technology go hand in hand. In this narrative, federated learning isn't just a technical term; it's the protagonist in safeguarding financial privacy, a tale where technology empowers consumers, giving them peace of mind as they navigate the digital marketplace.

FEATURE EXTRACTION

DEFINITION

Feature extraction in AI is identifying and selecting key pieces of information from raw data that are most relevant for problem-solving.

FEATURE EXTRACTION EXPLAINED

Think of feature extraction like a master chef preparing a complex dish. Just as the chef picks out the freshest ingredients or the most flavorful spices to create a culinary masterpiece, feature extraction in AI involves picking out the most essential bits of data to help a computer program understand and solve a problem. It's the art of sifting through a mountain of information — from the colors in a digital photo to the tone of a voice message — and plucking out the details that matter most. This selective process is crucial because it simplifies the vast data into digestible, insightful pieces, allowing AI to learn, adapt, and make decisions more efficiently.

A FEATURE EXTRACTION EXAMPLE

In the vibrant, eclectic world of online retail, where every click and hover holds meaning, an emerging fashion giant, Trendify, has harnessed feature extraction to revolutionize the shopping experience. Amidst the digital racks of clothing and accessories, Trendify's AI sifts through the chaos of data to personalize the fashion journey for millions.

This story begins not with a shopper but with data—vast arrays of it. Every image uploaded to Trendify's platform is a mix of colors, textures, and styles. The AI, acting almost like a discerning stylist, uses feature extraction to identify patterns and details: a fabric's drape, a dress's cut, and the season's palette. These aren't just images; they're a nuanced language of style that the AI learns to speak.

The result is a curated visual opportunity for shoppers. The site remembers when somebody with a penchant for polka dots scrolls through Trendify. It learns. The next time they log in, the algorithm presents them with a precise selection that seems handpicked by a personal shopper.

FUZZY LOGIC

DEFINITION

Fuzzy logic is a form of many-valued logic that deals with approximate rather than fixed and exact reasoning. Fuzzy logic variables may have a truth value between 0 and 1, representing the degree of truth.

FUZZY LOGIC EXPLAINED

Fuzzy logic handles the concept of partial truth, where the truth value may range between entirely true and completely false. It's beneficial in systems where human reasoning and decision-making, such as interpreting vague or imprecise data, are challenging to model with the precision of binary logic.

A FUZZY LOGIC EXPLAINED

Imagine navigating a ship through thick fog with limited visibility. Traditional navigation systems rely on precise data points. But what if the data is fuzzy, like "low visibility" or "somewhat close to shore"? This is where fuzzy logic comes in. Rolls-Royce, a global leader in marine propulsion systems, has incorporated fuzzy logic into their autopilot systems. These systems can interpret imprecise sensor data, like radar readings muffled by fog, and translate them into steering decisions. The fuzzy logic system essentially mimics human reasoning in uncertain situations, allowing ships to navigate safely through low-visibility conditions. This technology has demonstrably reduced the risk of collisions and groundings in challenging maritime environments.

GENERATIVE ADVERSARIAL NETWORKS (GANS)

DEFINITION

A class of machine learning frameworks in which two neural networks compete to generate new, synthetic data instances that can pass for real data.

GAN EXPLAINED

GANs involve two neural networks, the creator and the critic, working against each other. The creator endeavors to make new data, like images, look real, while the critic judges whether they're real or fake. Over time, the creator gets better at producing realistic data. It's like a forger trying to create a perfect painting that even an expert can't tell is fake.

A GAN EXAMPLE

The fashion industry witnessed a digital revolution with the introduction of GANs by designers like The Fabricant. This digital fashion house, pioneering GANs, created an innovation wave by auctioning a digital dress, "The Iridescence," entirely crafted through this AI technology. The dress, existing only in the digital realm, was superimposed on a photograph of the buyer, fitting perfectly to her form as if woven from the very pixels of the image itself.

This venture demonstrates how GANs can create highly realistic and intricate designs, opening new avenues for sustainable fashion, personal expression, and even ownership in a digital age.

GENETIC ALGORITHMS

DEFINITION

Genetic algorithms are search heuristics in AI that mimic natural evolution. They use selection, crossover, and mutation to evolve solutions to problems.

GENETIC ALGORITHMS EXPLAINED

Imagine a gaggle of robots trying to paint the Mona Lisa. They start with random brush strokes, most of which look nothing like the iconic image. But a few, by chance, resemble a corner of Da Vinci's masterpiece. These 'fitter' paintings are kept, while the rest are discarded. The robots then mix elements of these better attempts, perhaps the curve of a smile or the hint of an eyebrow, to create new paintings. Over many generations, with constant tweaking and combining, the robotic artists get closer to the original. Genetic algorithms operate on the same principle — they mix the best solutions from a set of attempts.

A GENETIC ALGORITHMS EXAMPLE

Imagine sifting through millions of potential drug combinations to find the one that eradicates a disease with minimal side effects. That's the daunting task facing pharmaceutical companies. But Pfizer, a leading pharmaceutical giant, is utilizing genetic algorithms (GAs) to revolutionize drug discovery.

GAs mimic the process of natural selection, where successful traits are passed on. In this case, Pfizer translates potential drug properties into a digital code. The GA then iterates through countless combinations, discarding ineffective ones and favoring those with desirable traits.

This approach has proven fruitful. Pfizer's GA-powered research led to the development of a successful new medication for a rare form of blood cancer. While GAs haven't replaced traditional methods entirely, they act as a powerful tool, accelerating drug discovery and offering a glimpse into the future of personalized medicine.

GENERATIVE AI

DEFINITION

Generative AI refers to artificial intelligence algorithms capable of creating content, such as text, images, videos, and music, that resembles human-generated content. It leverages advanced models to generate new data similar to but not identical to the data it was trained on, enabling a wide range of creative and analytical applications.

GENERATIVE AI EXPLAINED

Generative AI is like an imaginative artist with a mind of silicon and circuits. It's a type of artificial intelligence that doesn't just understand data; it uses that understanding to create new, original content—from poetry to pictures that could pass for a human's work. This type of AI learns from existing music, literature, or images, grasping the underlying patterns. Then, like a composer dreaming up a new magnum opus, it generates original works that echo the style it learned from but with a new twist. The results can be stunning: a machine dreaming up fashions that grace digital runways or painting virtual landscapes indistinguishable from the real thing. Generative AI isn't just copying; it's re-imagining.

A GENERATIVE AI EXAMPLE

A technology startup called Artisto harnessed generative AI to revolutionize the graphic design industry. Their platform allows users to input basic design preferences and textual descriptions, which the AI then uses to create sophisticated, ready-to-use digital artwork and design concepts.

"Artisto's" platform significantly democratized design, enabling small businesses and individuals without formal design training to produce professional-quality visuals for marketing, branding, and content creation. The AI's ability to generate a wide range of styles and adapt to specific user inputs led to widespread acclaim, with the startup being featured in design innovation showcases and tech news outlets.

Chapter Five

FROM H TO L

HEURISTIC SEARCH

DEFINITION

Heuristic search is a problem-solving approach that uses practical methods or shortcuts to discover by trial and error and educated guesses rather than following a strict procedure. It's used to find a satisfactory solution where finding an optimal solution is impractical due to time constraints.

HEURISTIC SEARCH EXPLAINED

Heuristic search is akin to an experienced detective using gut instincts to crack a case. Instead of combing through every clue with equal scrutiny, this method applies clever shortcuts and educated guesses to find solutions more quickly. Imagine a vast library of books, and you're searching for one with a blue cover; a heuristic search wouldn't meticulously check every book; instead, it'd guide you to sections where blue covers are most likely found, significantly speeding up the search. In AI, this approach helps computers solve complex problems efficiently by focusing on the most promising paths, sidestepping the need to explore every possible option. This blend of intuition and logic enables machines to tackle tasks like finding the shortest route on a map or winning a game of chess, making heuristic search a critical tool in the AI toolkit for navigating the labyrinth of decision-making.

A HEURISTIC SEARCH EXAMPLE

In the competitive mobile gaming arena, GameGenius introduced an innovative way to enhance player engagement using heuristic search algorithms. Their flagship game, "Puzzle Quest," a complex labyrinth of challenges and adventures, was notorious for its difficulty levels, often leaving players stuck and frustrated.

GameGenius deployed a heuristic search to analyze player behavior data, identifying patterns and stumbling blocks within the game. This smart algorithm acted as a virtual game master, subtly adjusting the difficulty level and suggesting strategies tailored to individual player styles. Instead of offering one-size-fits-all solutions, it provided hints and pathways based on the player's past decisions, making each suggestion feel personal and intuitive.

This early application of heuristic search resulted in a more fluid game flow with tough but not insurmountable challenges. Users praised the game for its engaging yet accessible puzzles, and the feedback was overwhelmingly positive.

HUMAN IN THE LOOP (HITL)

DEFINITION

Human in the Loop (HITL) is an AI development approach that integrates human judgment into the AI's learning process, ensuring accuracy, ethical decision-making, and continuous improvement.

HUMAN IN THE LOOP EXPLAINED

Imagine AI as a student and humans as mentors, where the machine learns not in isolation but under our guidance. This approach ensures that AI systems don't just race ahead, making decisions based on data alone; they pause, reflect, and learn from human feedback, blending the best of both worlds. It's like having a safety net that catches mistakes and biases, making AI more reliable and trustworthy. Whether screening job applications or moderating online content, HITL keeps the human touch alive in digital decisions, ensuring that technology serves us in ethical, accurate, and continuously improving ways. In a landscape where machines learn to mimic human intelligence, HITL reaffirms the value of human judgment, steering AI towards a more balanced and beneficial future.

A HUMAN IN THE LOOP EXAMPLE

Waymo, a pioneer in self-driving car technology, has long envisioned a future of autonomous vehicles navigating our streets seamlessly. However, their journey has been riddled with challenges, highlighting the importance of Human-in-the-Loop (HITL) systems.

In a recent incident, Waymo's self-driving taxis encountered unexpected situations that confused their AI systems. The cars became overly cautious, halting in the middle of traffic. Thankfully, human backup drivers, constantly monitoring the vehicles through a HITL system, were able to intervene and take control, preventing accidents.

This episode underscores the limitations of current self-driving technology and the crucial role humans still play in ensuring safety. Waymo continues to refine its AI systems, but the incident serves as a reminder that for now, a human hand remains firmly on the wheel, ready to hit the brakes when the AI gets in over its head.

IOT (INTERNET OF THINGS)

DEFINITION

IoT refers to the worldwide collection of physical objects—"things"—that contain embedded sensors, software, and other emerging technologies that can connect and exchange data with other devices and systems connected via the Internet.

IOT EXPLAINED

Picture a world where your fridge can order milk before you run out, your thermostat adjusts the temperature based on your preferences, and your car warns you about upcoming maintenance—all without human intervention. This is the Internet of Things (IoT). It's a network of devices, from everyday household items to sophisticated industrial tools, all interconnected and communicating. These devices collect and share data, making everything more connected, efficient, and smart. However, this connectivity also opens up new vulnerabilities, making security a paramount concern in the IoT universe.

AN IOT EXAMPLE

Imagine a vast network of sensors monitoring every aspect of a farm, from soil moisture to cow health. This isn't science fiction; it's the reality of IoT (Internet of Things) in agriculture.

Dutch dairy giant FrieslandCampina equips its farms with a network of IoT sensors that track everything from cow activity to milk quality. The real-time data allows farmers to optimize feed schedules, detect early signs of illness in cows, and ensure optimal growing conditions for crops.

This IoT-powered approach has resulted in healthier cows, increased milk yield, and reduced waste. Spoiled lettuce due to improper storage? IoT sensors can monitor temperatures in warehouses and shipping containers, preventing spoilage and ensuring fresh produce reaches consumers. The IoT is transforming agriculture from a traditional practice to a data-driven industry, boosting efficiency, sustainability, and food security.

KNOWLEDGE REPRESENTATION

DEFINITION

Knowledge representation is a method in AI for structuring information and rules about the world. It can be in various forms, such as semantic networks, ontologies, and rules, to structure information in ways that make it usable for reasoning and decision-making.

KNOWLEDGE REPRESENTATION EXPLAINED

Imagine trying to explain the rules of a board game to a robot so it can play against you. Knowledge representation is essentially that, but on a grander scale. It's how scientists teach computers to understand our world by breaking down complex concepts, facts, and rules into a language that machines can grasp. This method allows computers to navigate through mazes of information, make sense of it, and even make decisions or solve problems, much like a detective piecing together clues to solve a mystery. Whether diagnosing a rare disease or predicting weather patterns, knowledge representation is the foundation that helps AI understand and interact with the real world. It bridges human knowledge and machine intelligence, enabling computers to calculate reason and learn.

A KNOWLEDGE REPRESENTATION EXAMPLE

In the cultivated vineyards of Bordeaux, where tradition meets innovation, Château DataVine embarked on a digital transformation journey, leveraging knowledge representation to revolutionize wine production. This centuries-old vineyard, renowned for its exquisite blends, integrated AI to enhance the quality and consistency of its wines, preserving the legacy of craftsmanship while embracing the future.

The challenge was formidable: how to encapsulate seasoned winemakers' vast, nuanced expertise into a form that computers could understand and use? The solution lay in knowledge representation, a method that translated the complex wine-making variables—soil quality, grape variety, weather patterns, and fermentation processes—into a structured digital knowledge base. This AI system, fed with generations of winemaking wisdom, could predict the optimal harvest time, adjust fermentation conditions, and even recommend blending ratios to achieve the perfect vintage.

LARGE LANGUAGE MODELS (LLMS)

DEFINITION

Large language models (LLMs) are advanced AI models trained on vast amounts of text data. They understand and generate human-like text and can perform a wide range of language-based tasks without task-specific training.

LLM EXPLAINED

LLMs like GPT (Generative Pre-trained Transformer) have revolutionized natural language processing by providing nuanced understanding and generation of human language. They're used in applications such as writing essays, translating languages, summarizing articles or long texts, and generating code in various computer languages, making them versatile tools for multiple applications. Their ability to understand context and develop coherent, contextually relevant text has opened new possibilities in AI-driven content creation, customer service, and more.

AN LLM EXAMPLE

In the bustling world of publishing, where the written word is both art and commerce, a ground-breaking collaboration emerged between ScriboTech, an innovative software company, and Alexandria Publishing House, a guardian of literary tradition. Together, they embarked on an ambitious project to re-imagine storytelling with the help of large language models (LLMs).

The project, dubbed "The Next Chapter," aimed to harness the capabilities of LLMs to co-create novels with human authors. These advanced AI models, trained on vast text libraries, could generate narrative suggestions, plot twists, and character dialogues, offering writers a unique blend of inspiration and efficiency.

One standout success was "Elysium's Echo," a science fiction novel co-authored by AI and celebrated novelist Elena M. The collaboration showcased the LLM's ability to weave intricate storylines and richly imagined worlds, while Elena brought emotional depth and human touch to the narrative.

"51 ESSENTIAL AI TERMS EXPLAINED FOR LEADERS" REVIEW PAGE

"If your actions inspire others to dream more, learn more, do more and become more, you are a leader."
~ John Quincy Adams

We hope that you are finding the book useful. I suspect that there are many other leaders out there, who were like you used to be. Less experienced, needing answers, but not sure who or what to trust.

Most people do, in fact, judge a book by its cover (and its reviews). So here's my request to you as an amazing leader who I know is committed to helping others succeed.

Please help that leader by leaving this book a review.

It's remarkably hassle-free, it doesn't cost you anything, it will take about 60 seconds and your review really could help.

If you are **on audible** - hit the three dots in the top right of your device, click rate & review, then leave a few sentences about the book with a star rating.

If you are reading on **kindle, iPad or other tablet** - scroll to the bottom of the book, then swipe up and it will prompt a review for you.

If for some reason these are working for you, then go to Amazon and leave a review right **on the book's page**. Here's

the link:
https://www.amazon.com/review/review-your-purchases/?asin=1917220006

If all fails, **scan this QR code**:

Thank you for doing that. It makes more of a difference to the next leader who may be considering whether to get this book

than you realize.

Right, let's get back to the main event. On with more of those essential AI terms, definitions and explanations.

Thank you so much

Marco Ryan
London, March 2024

Chapter Six

FROM M TO N

MACHINE LEARNING (ML)

DEFINITION

A subset of AI that enables computers to learn from and make decisions based on data without being explicitly programmed for each task.

MACHINE LEARNING EXPLAINED

Machine learning is like teaching a child through experience. Instead of programming a computer to perform every possible action, machine learning allows it to learn from examples. You provide data (the examples), and the computer analyzes this data to understand patterns or rules. Over time

A MACHINE LEARNING EXAMPLE

In the aviation sector, where safety is paramount and the margin for error is razor-thin, Airbus took a bold leap with its pioneering project, Skywise. Launched in 2017, Skywise aimed to harness the power of machine learning to transform aircraft maintenance, predicting potential issues before they could become problems.

Skywise integrates machine learning algorithms to analyze vast amounts of operational and performance data collected from aircraft operated by its customers around the globe, including the many airlines that are its customers. This ability to access data at scale, often in real-time, enables the system to identify patterns and anomalies that human analysts might overlook, predict potential failures, and suggest preemptive maintenance actions.

The impact of Airbus's innovation became palpably clear when one of its airline partners reported a remarkable reduction in unscheduled aircraft maintenance. This not only enhanced the fleet's reliability but also significantly improved operational efficiency and safety, ensuring that passengers reached their destinations without delay or disruption.

NATURAL LANGUAGE GENERATION (NLG)

DEFINITION

A subfield of artificial intelligence that transforms structured data into natural language. It enables computers to generate human-like text based on data inputs.

NLG EXPLAINED

NLG involves the automatic creation of text that is indistinguishable from that written by humans. It's used in report generation, customer service, and content creation, providing a way to automatically produce narratives from data, making information more accessible and understandable for humans. It differs from Natural Language Processing, which is concerned with understanding incoming language input, whereas NLG focuses on producing language output that humans can understand. Both work together in sophisticated AI systems to facilitate seamless human-machine interactions.

AN NLG EXAMPLE

In the fast-paced world of news, where every second counts, the Associated Press embarked on a digital revolution that would redefine the landscape of journalism. In 2014, the venerable news organization, in partnership with Automated Insights, introduced an AI-driven system powered by NLG technology to automate the production of financial reports.

This bold move was born out of necessity. The Associated Press, responsible for delivering news quickly and accurately to a global audience, faced the daunting task of reporting on over 4,000 companies' quarterly earnings. With NLG, the Associated Press transformed raw financial data into coherent, ready-to-publish news stories at an unprecedented scale and speed.

The technology didn't just work; it excelled. By automating routine financial reports, the journalists were freed to focus on in-depth analysis, investigative reporting, and storytelling— tasks that require a more human touch. The NLG system generated reports indistinguishable from those written by human reporters, producing thousands of articles on quarterly earnings each year.

NATURAL LANGUAGE PROCESSING (NLP)

DEFINITION

A branch of AI that enables computers to understand, interpret, and respond to human language meaningfully.

NLP EXPLAINED

Imagine conversing with someone who speaks a different language yet understands each other perfectly. That's the magic of Natural Language Processing (NLP), a branch of artificial intelligence that helps machines understand human language. It's not just about recognizing words; NLP allows computers to grasp the nuances of human communication, like sarcasm, humor, and context, turning them into something they can process. This technology powers your daily digital assistants, translates languages in real time, and even sifts through mountains of data to find the necessary information. From asking your phone for weather updates to getting recommendations from a chatbot, NLP is the unsung hero, making these interactions feel natural. It's bridging the gap between human complexity and digital simplicity, making technology more accessible and intuitive for everyone.

A NLP EXAMPLE

In the hushed corridors of the legal world, tradition and caution are by words, and the pace of innovation is often measured in years and decades. Yet in 2015, a new tool named "ROSS Intelligence" promised to transform the laborious task of legal research.

Developed with the power of Natural Language Processing (NLP), ROSS was designed to do what had always seemed to be such a Herculean task: transform how lawyers conduct research, making it faster, more accurate, and intuitive.

With a simple query in plain English, akin to asking a colleague, lawyers could now uncover relevant case precedents, interpretations, and legal arguments in a fraction of the time it once took. The platform, leveraging NLP, understood the context of their questions, parsed through millions of legal documents, and presented answers that were once buried in mountains of text.

The impact was immediate and profound. Lawyers previously shackled by the laborious process of traditional legal research were now free to take on more cases, delve deeper into legal analysis, and serve their clients with unprecedented efficiency.

NEURAL NETWORKS

DEFINITION

Neural networks computational models inspired by the human brain's structure and function are designed to recognize patterns and solve complex problems by processing information through layers of interconnected nodes, or "neurons."

NEURAL NETWORKS EXPLAINED

Your brain is a bustling hub of neurons working tirelessly to process every thought, decision, and memory. Neural networks attempt to mimic this intricate web of human cognition, albeit on a digital stage. These networks are collections of algorithms designed to recognize patterns, interpret data, and learn from them, much like how we know from experience. By simulating the way neurons interact in the human brain, Neural networks enable machines to tackle tasks that require a human-like understanding, which has opened a world in which technology not only computes but perceives and reacts to the world around it in ways once thought to be the exclusive domain of humans. Whether it's understanding spoken words, recommending your next favorite song, or identifying a friend in a photo, neural networks are the unseen workers behind the face of AI.

A NEURAL NETWORK EXAMPLE

Remember AlphaGo, the AI program that dominated the world of Go, an ancient complex strategy game? Developed by DeepMind, a subsidiary of Google, AlphaGo's successor, AlphaGo Zero, took things a step further. This program wasn't trained on human games; it learned solely by playing against itself, using neural networks to develop superhuman strategies. While seemingly unrelated to medicine, AlphaGo Zero's underlying technology holds immense potential for drug discovery.

Pharmaceutical companies like GlaxoSmithKline (GSK) are utilizing similar neural networks to navigate the vast chemical space in search of new drug candidates. These networks can analyze complex molecular structures and identify potential drug targets, a process traditionally slow and laborious.

By mimicking AlphaGo Zero's self-learning approach, researchers can explore uncharted territories in the world of molecules, accelerating the discovery of life-saving medications. This is just one example of how neural networks, inspired by the human brain's learning ability, are poised to revolutionize the pharmaceutical industry.

ONTOLOGIES

DEFINITION

Ontologies are structured frameworks for organizing information and defining concepts' types, properties, and interrelationships within a domain to enable clear communication, data integration, and knowledge sharing across systems and with users.

ONTOLOGIES EXPLAINED

Picture a vast library where every book, no matter the topic, is meticulously organized, making it effortless for anyone to find exactly what they're looking for. In the digital world, ontologies serve a similar purpose for artificial intelligence (AI). They create a structured roadmap of knowledge, categorizing and connecting concepts in a way AI systems can understand. Whether it's medical research, online shopping, or exploring your inner Stephen Hawking, ontologies help AI navigate diverse subjects precisely. It's like giving AI a guidebook to the world's knowledge, enabling it to communicate more naturally with us, make smarter decisions, and even discover new insights by seeing the links between seemingly unrelated pieces of information. As such, ontologies are the backbone of AI's understanding.

AN ONTOLOGIES EXAMPLE

Biodiversity loss is one of the most pressing challenges of our time. EcoNet, a coalition of environmental researchers and Silicon Valley tech pioneers, has been formed to address the issue directly. EcoNet leverages the power of ontologies to tackle biodiversity loss.

EcoNet's mission began with the ambitious goal of creating a unified, digital encyclopedia of all known species, their habitats, behaviors, and the ecological dynamics that bind them. This monumental task was akin to mapping a vast, uncharted territory where every organism is a piece of a larger puzzle.

By employing ontologies, EcoNet structured this immense volume of data into a coherent system, categorizing relationships between species and their environments in a way that both machines and humans could understand. This structured knowledge network became vital for scientists and policymakers, offering unprecedented insights into conservation strategies, habitat preservation, and climate change impacts.

EcoNet's success illustrates the transformative potential of ontologies in understanding our natural world. Through its digital lens, we gain a clearer view of the intricate web of life, empowering us to protect our planet with informed, data-driven decisions. EcoNet's triumph showcases the game-changing role ontologies play in deciphering the complexities of the natural environment. Such structured knowledge is invaluable in environmental management and policy-making, allowing us to approach conservation and sustainability efforts with precision and foresight.

Chapter Seven

FROM P TO R

PREDICTIVE ANALYTICS

DEFINITION

A set of tools for analyzing large quantities of historical data and then forecasting upcoming patterns. The more complete the data affecting the outcomes, the more accurate the forecast will be.

PREDICTIVE ANALYTICS EXPLAINED

Imagine if you could peek into a crystal ball and see the future, not just to predict the weather or the outcome of a sports game, but to foresee complex events, like market trends or health risks. That's the power of Predictive Analytics, a futuristic tool in the AI toolkit. It sifts through mountains of data—past sales, customer behavior, weather patterns—to find hidden patterns and use them to predict what might happen next. It's like having a time machine, but instead of traveling to the future, you bring future insights back to the present. Companies use it to decide which products to stock, hospitals use it to prevent diseases, and cities use it to plan for traffic.

A PREDICTIVE ANALYTICS EXAMPLE

In the heart of America's Midwest, the agricultural giant John Deere sowed the seeds of a revolution, not in the fields but in the data centers, where predictive analytics germinated into a tool as vital as the tractor. In 2017, John Deere acquired Blue River Technology, supercharging its leap into the future of farming with AI-driven predictive analytics.

Blue River's "See & Spray" technology epitomizes this transformation. Traditional methods blanket crops with water, nutrients, and pesticides, often wastefully. See & Spray, however, employs cameras and machine learning to scrutinize plants as they pass beneath the equipment, discerning crops from weeds. Predictive analytics then enable precise pesticide application to the weeds alone, boosting yield while minimizing environmental impact.

The benefits were immediate and profound: an astounding 90% reduction in herbicide use, healthier crops, and lower farmer costs. John Deere's foray into predictive analytics not only redefined sustainable farming practices but also demonstrated how data, when harnessed through AI, can cultivate a greener future.

PROMPT ENGINEERING

DEFINITION

Prompt engineering involves crafting inputs (prompts) to effectively communicate with AI models, especially large language models (LLMs), to generate desired outputs. It's a skill that blends creativity, understanding of the AI's capabilities, and strategic thinking to elicit high-quality responses from AI systems.

PROMPT ENGINEERING EXPLAINED

Think of Prompt engineering as the art of conversation with a machine, where the quality of your question can dramatically shape the AI's answer. This technique is crucial because AI, much like a keen but literal-minded apprentice, thrives on clear, well-structured instructions to produce insightful, accurate, and relevant outputs. Prompt engineering becomes a bridge, guiding the AI to understand the letter and the spirit of your inquiry, ensuring the interaction is as fruitful and precise as possible. It's a dance of words and intent, where every step—the prompt—leads the AI in the direction we wish to explore, unlocking the full potential of these digital minds in a wide array of tasks.

PROMPT ENGINEERING EXAMPLE

In the bustling advertising world, where the right message can make or break a campaign, the creative agency "AdCrafters" stumbled upon a novel solution in 2021 that would set their content apart: prompt engineering for AI-generated copy. Facing the challenge of crafting fresh, engaging ads for "EcoBrew," a rising star in sustainable coffee, AdCrafters employed AI with language capabilities to generate ad copy that resonated with environmentally conscious consumers.

The magic lay in how AdCrafters' team became prompt engineers—designing precise, thought-provoking prompts that guided the AI to produce not just any content but copy that spoke directly to the hearts of EcoBrew's audience. The results were astonishing: ads that blended creativity with a deep understanding of EcoBrew's mission, driving engagement and sales to new heights.

QUANTUM COMPUTING

DEFINITION

An area of computing focused on developing computer technology - both hardware and algorithms – that exploits the principles of quantum mechanics to solve highly complex problems that traditional computers would never be able to solve quickly.

QUANTUM COMPUTING EXPLAINED

Quantum computing is a leap into the future of technology, harnessing the bizarre, counterintuitive principles of quantum mechanics to process information in ways that traditional computers can't fathom. Unlike classical computing, which relies on bits (0s and 1s) to perform calculations, quantum computing uses quantum bits or qubits. These qubits can exist in multiple states at once and can be entangled with each other, allowing quantum computers to perform complex calculations at breakneck speeds. To give you an analogy: Classic computing is a bit like trying to find the right key for a lock. The computer tries each key in turn until it finds the right one that opens the lock. The equivalent in Quantum Computing is that the computer inserts all the keys at once into identical locks, and turn the keys at the same instance, noting which one is successful. Quantum Computing promises to revolutionize fields ranging from cryptography to drug discovery, solving problems in seconds that would take conventional computers millennia to crack,

A QUANTUM COMPUTING EXAMPLE

In the search for cleaner energy sources, Volkswagen AG turned to quantum computing to tackle the enormous challenge of traffic optimization in metropolitan areas. In 2019, Volkswagen and Google announced a collaboration that utilized quantum computing's formidable power to reduce urban congestion and emissions.

Their first real-world test unfolded in Lisbon, Portugal; Volkswagen's quantum computing algorithm analyzed public bus routes, factoring in variables like traffic, stops, and transfers to devise a more efficient transportation flow. The result was a dynamic routing plan that adapted in real-time to traffic conditions, significantly reducing waiting times, improving bus capacities, and cutting emissions by optimizing routes.

RECOMMENDER SYSTEMS

DEFINITION

Recommender systems are algorithms used by websites and apps to suggest products, services, or content to users based on their past behaviors, preferences, and similar users' data.

RECOMMENDER SYSTEMS EXPLAINED

Recommender systems are like the digital version of your best friend who knows your tastes so well they can predict what movie you'll love next or the perfect gift for your mom. These systems analyze your past choices, combine this with what they know from others with similar tastes, and then suggest options you'll likely enjoy. Whether it's the next binge-worthy series on a streaming platform, a product on an online shopping site, or a song on a music app, recommender systems are the unseen matchmakers of the digital world. They make navigating the vast sea of options online manageable and surprisingly personal, tailoring the Internet to each user's unique preferences.

A RECOMMENDER SYSTEMS EXAMPLE

Thanks to its pioneering use of recommender systems, Netflix has become synonymous with personalized viewing experiences. Since shifting to streaming in 2007, Netflix has leveraged complex algorithms to suggest shows and movies to millions of subscribers worldwide, fundamentally changing how people discover content.

The secret sauce of Netflix's success lies in its sophisticated recommender system, which analyzes vast amounts of data from user interactions—what you've watched, searched for, or rated—to predict what else you might like. But it doesn't stop there. The system also considers the behavior of users with similar tastes, creating a network of recommendations that feel surprisingly personal.

This innovative approach to content discovery has kept viewers glued to their screens and redefined the entertainment landscape. By 2015, Netflix reported that its recommendation engine was worth $1 billion annually, highlighting the economic value of keeping subscribers engaged and reducing churn.

REINFORCEMENT LEARNING

DEFINITION

Reinforcement learning is a type of machine learning in which an algorithm learns to make decisions by taking actions in an environment to achieve some goals.

REINFORCEMENT LEARNING EXPLAINED

Reinforcement learning is like dog training that uses treats and commands. In this AI training method, the computer program, or "agent," learns to achieve a goal in an uncertain, potentially complex environment. It works through trial and error, receiving "treats" or rewards for actions that move it closer to the desired outcome. Incorrect actions lead to no reward or a "penalty," guiding the agent to adjust its strategy. Over time, the agent learns the best actions to take, much like a dog learns to sit or stay. This learning process enables AI to master everything from video games to driving cars by understanding the consequences of its actions and refining its approach to maximize the "treats" or rewards.

A REINFORCEMENT LEARNING EXAMPLE

In logistics, the multinational delivery service FedEx utilized reinforcement learning to navigate the complex management of its shipping network. In 2018, FedEx implemented an AI system that uses reinforcement learning to optimize delivery routes, considering traffic patterns, weather conditions, and package volumes. This solution doesn't just follow pre-programmed instructions; it constantly learns and adapts, improving its decision-making with every package delivered.

The results were staggering. FedEx reported increased efficiency, significantly reducing fuel consumption, and improved delivery times. In Memphis alone, route optimizations led to a 10% cut in travel distance. This isn't just a tale of corporate profit but of environmental stewardship and customer satisfaction, illustrating how reinforcement learning can drive not just vehicles but change, paving the way to a more sustainable and punctual delivery service.

ROBOTICS

DEFINITION

Robotics is the engineering field concerned with the design, construction, operation, and application of robots, machines capable of automatically carrying out a complex series of actions.

ROBOTICS EXPLAINED

Robotics is a blend of science, engineering, and technology that creates machines, known as robots, designed to perform tasks that humans either can't or prefer not to do. It encompasses the physical design and manufacturing of these robots and the algorithms that drive their autonomy. These tasks range from assembling cars on a production line to exploring the ocean's depths. Robotics combines mechanical structures with computer systems to enable robots to process information and make decisions, allowing them to interact with the physical world. Through robotics, we're developing companions that can assist in everything from mundane household chores to complex space expeditions, fundamentally reshaping the landscape of human capabilities.

A ROBOTICS EXAMPLE

In the vineyards of France, robotics took on an unexpectedly traditional role. At Château Clerc Milon, part of Baron Philippe de Rothschild's wine estates, a robot named 'Ted' was introduced in 2018 to plow the vineyards. Ted, designed by Naïo Technologies, revolutionized vineyard maintenance. It operated autonomously, navigating between rows of grapevines, tilling the soil, and managing weeds without chemical herbicides.

What made Ted exceptional was its precision and consistency, reducing soil compaction, a side effect of traditional tractor plowing, thereby promoting healthier vine growth and grape quality. It marked a foray into sustainable viticulture, integrating eco-friendly technology with traditional wine-making practices.

Chapter Eight

JUST THE LETTER S

SEMANTIC ANALYSIS

DEFINITION

Semantic analysis in AI is the process by which a computer system discerns meaning from language, grasping the context, emotions, and intentions behind the words it uses.

SEMANTIC ANALYSIS EXPLAINED

Semantic analysis is like reading between the lines, a skill AI uses to understand human language not just by words but also by context and significance. It allows a computer to recognize that when someone says, "I'm feeling blue," they're expressing sadness, not literally turning a different shade of color. This understanding goes beyond mere dictionary definitions, delving into culture, tone, and nuance. Semantic analysis enables AI to interpret text from a human-like perspective, considering the subtleties and complexities of language. It's a cornerstone of technologies like voice assistants and chatbots, which rely on this capability to interact with users in a meaningful and relevant way.

A SEMANTIC ANALYSIS EXAMPLE

Semantic analysis found an unexpected home in the UK supermarket chain Tesco. In 2016, Tesco implemented a customer feedback system powered by semantic analysis to decipher the vast array of customer reviews and feedback left across various platforms.

Tesco has been a pioneer of data-driven customer service since buying the data company DunHumby when most supermarkets were trying to acquire each other. DunHumby. Gave them the data analysis tools and skills to look for patterns and nuance in customer buying behaviors facilitated by their loyalty card – the Tesco Club Card. On these solid data foundations, Tesco then deployed AI – in this case, Semantic Analysis. The solution didn't tally up positive and negative words. It understood context. Compliments on "fresh" fish signified satisfaction, while "fresh" regarding the checkout experience hinted at frustrations over delays. By interpreting these subtleties, Tesco could derive actionable insights, leading to tailored improvements in customer service and product offerings.

SEMANTIC WEB

DEFINITION

The Semantic Web is an extension of the World Wide Web that enables computers to understand and interpret data on the Web as humans do through standards and formats that provide meaning to information.

THE SEMANTIC WEB EXPLAINED

The Semantic Web isn't just about putting more data on the web. It's about making that data understandable for machines. It uses a special code that helps computers "read" and use the web more intelligently and meaningfully for human users. Think of it like this: If the current web is a foreign language that computers can only mimic, the Semantic Web is the equivalent of giving them a fluency course, allowing them to understand the subtleties and nuances of human language. This doesn't just make searching for information more efficient; it transforms the web into a space where data is interlinked, and knowledge is shared seamlessly, paving the way for smarter search engines, automation services, and AI applications that can work with us to solve complex problems.

A SEMANTIC WEB EXAMPLE

In the world of library science, an industry that may seem as old as the written word itself, the Semantic Web spun a new narrative. The British Library, one of the largest libraries in the world, took on the herculean task of modernizing access to its vast collection. In 2020, it began implementing Semantic Web technologies to make its digital records more accessible and inter-operable.

By structuring meta-data according to Semantic Web standards, the British Library enabled machines to understand the "aboutness" of a book, article, or manuscript. This wasn't just about digital cataloging; it was about weaving a web of context around every item in their collection, from a 15th-century illuminated manuscript to the latest scientific periodicals. Researchers could now traverse a digital landscape where resources were linked by meaning, not just by keywords or authors. The Semantic Web turned the British Library's catalog into a navigable universe of knowledge, where a query about Shakespeare yielded his works and connected to adaptations, reviews, and academic research, revolutionizing how we access and engage with the fabric of human knowledge.

SENTIMENT ANALYSIS

DEFINITION

Sentiment analysis, also known as opinion mining, is a field of AI that interprets and classifies people's emotions within text data, categorizing opinions expressed as positive, negative, or neutral.

SENTIMENT ANALYSIS EXPLAINED

Sentiment analysis is essentially AI developing emotional intelligence. It's the technology behind a computer's ability to sift through tweets, reviews, or conversations and understand whether the writer feels happy, angry, or indifferent about a subject. This goes beyond just spotting happy or sad emojis; it involves detecting sarcasm, context, and subtleties of language. This powerful tool is used by businesses to gauge public opinion, by politicians to understand voter sentiment, or by product developers to listen to customer feedback. Sentiment analysis transforms online communication's vast, chaotic world into structured, actionable insights.

A SENTIMENT ANALYSIS EXAMPLE

Fast food might seem like an unlikely contender for sentiment analysis, but it brought McDonald's a feast of insights. In 2019, the fast-food giant started using sentiment analysis to mine social media and customer feedback, not just to count complaints or compliments but to understand the emotions behind them. This deep dive into customer sentiment helped McDonald's tailor its menu and services to better meet diners' needs.

For instance, when sentiment analysis revealed that customers were ecstatic about the convenience of digital ordering kiosks but frustrated with wait times during peak hours, McDonald's responded by optimizing staffing and kitchen operations. The result was a significant improvement in service speed and customer satisfaction, reflected in both online sentiment and sales figures.

By tapping into sentiment analysis, McDonald's transformed the voices of its customers into a guiding star for business strategy. This showcased how AI can deliver more than just efficiency—it can deliver a deeper connection with customers.

SPEECH RECOGNITION

DEFINITION

Speech recognition technology allows computers to identify and process human voice, transforming spoken language into text or commands.

SPEECH RECOGNITION EXPLAINED

Speech recognition is the technology that allows our words to be heard and understood by machines, not with ears, but with algorithms. When you speak to your phone, and it answers or dictates a message that gets transcribed without a single keystroke—that's speech recognition in action. It's a complex blend of acoustic models that identify sounds, language models that interpret words, and machine learning that continuously improves accuracy. It's how devices can listen and respond to multiple languages and dialects, opening up a world where hands-free communication with technology is as natural as chatting with a friend.

A SPEECH RECOGNITION EXAMPLE

In the US, the rail operator Amtrak's virtual assistant, "Julie," revolutionized the way travelers got information. Introduced in the early 2000s, Julie was empowered with speech recognition capabilities to provide callers with train schedules, fares, and other essential travel information.

The voice of Amtrak, Julie, was initially designed to field simple inquiries, but as speech recognition technology advanced, so did her abilities. By 2012, Julie could handle more than 5 million calls a year, allowing customers to swiftly book tickets or get real-time updates just by speaking naturally.

SUPERVISED LEARNING

DEFINITION

Supervised learning is a type of machine learning where algorithms learn from labeled training data and use this to predict outcomes or classify information.

SUPERVISED LEARNING EXPLAINED

Supervised learning is like teaching a child with flashcards. The flashcards (the training data) have pictures with names written on them (the labels), and over time, the child learns to associate the image with the correct word. In the digital realm, supervised learning works similarly. AI systems are fed large amounts of labeled data — for example, photos of cats labeled "cat." The system uses this to learn what a cat looks like. Later on, when it sees a new photo, it can recognize whether or not there's a cat in it. This method is widely used in applications such as email filtering, where the AI learns to identify which emails are spam and which are not based on examples it has been given.

A SUPERVISED LEARNING EXAMPLE

In 2015, supervised learning took center stage at Penfolds, one of the oldest wineries in the heartland of Australia's wine country. Faced with the challenge of sorting grapes based on quality, Penfolds turned to AI equipped with supervised learning capabilities. Cameras and sensors became the system's eyes, taking detailed images of the grapes as they passed on the conveyor belt.

The AI had been "taught" using thousands of photos of grapes previously sorted by experienced winemakers—good grapes labeled as such and poor ones likewise. This training enabled the AI to accurately assess the quality of grapes in real time, sorting them with a precision that matched the seasoned experts. The result was a marked improvement in the quality of the wine, with the system ensuring only the best grapes made it into Penfolds' vintages.

Chapter Nine

FROM MORE S TO T

SWARM INTELLIGENCE

DEFINITION

A field of artificial intelligence based on the collective behavior of decentralized, self-organized systems, natural or synthetic. The concept is employed in work on artificial intelligence. The expression was introduced by Gerardo Beni and Jing Wang in 1989 in the context of cellular robotic systems.

SWARM INTELLIGENCE EXPLAINED

At its core, Swarm Intelligence is about how simple creatures following simple rules can solve complex problems without a leader or blueprint. Imagine thousands of ants finding the shortest route to food or countless birds moving in sync to form mesmerizing patterns in the sky. These aren't random acts but the result of swarm intelligence, where the collective becomes smarter than its individual parts. This concept, borrowed from nature, is applied in artificial intelligence to create systems that can tackle complex tasks by mimicking these natural processes. By understanding local cues and following basic protocols, artificial agents can make decisions, optimize solutions, and adapt to changes, mirroring the natural world's resilience and efficiency.

A SWARM INTELLIGENCE EXAMPLE

In a clever initiative, researchers at the Swiss Federal Institute of Technology (ETH Zurich) have turned to Swarm Intelligence for environmental conservation, specifically in the monitoring and preserving of wildlife and their habitats. This project, known as the "Swarm Robotic Project," launched in the late 2010s, involves the use of small, autonomous robots designed to mimic the collective behavior of swarms found in nature, such as fish schools or bird flocks.

These robots, equipped with sensors and cameras, are deployed in natural habitats to collect data on wildlife populations, vegetation levels, and environmental conditions without disturbing the local ecosystem. Operating as a cohesive unit, these robots can cover vast areas more efficiently than traditional methods or single, larger robots could. Based on real-time data and the collective input from the swarm, they make decisions on the fly about where to go and what to monitor, ensuring comprehensive coverage and data collection.

This innovative approach has allowed for more effective monitoring of endangered species and their environments, providing conservationists with valuable insights into patterns of migration, population changes, and environmental threats. One of the project's notable successes has been its application in monitoring bird populations in remote areas, where the robots' ability to cover large distances and access rugged terrain has provided unprecedented data on bird migration patterns and habitat use.

SYMBOLIC AI

DEFINITION

Symbolic AI involves computers understanding and processing human knowledge and reasoning through symbols and rules rather than numerical data to make decisions and solve problems.

SYMBOLIC AI EXPLAINED

Symbolic AI, also known as "good old-fashioned AI," refers to the early days of artificial intelligence research, which focused on mimicking human thought processes and logic. Instead of learning from data like modern AI, Symbolic AI uses a system of symbols to represent objects and concepts, applying a set of rules to manipulate these symbols and derive conclusions or actions. This approach allows computers to perform tasks that require understanding complex relationships and reasoning, such as language translation or solving puzzles. By explicitly encoding knowledge and logic into a system, Symbolic AI attempts to create machines that can think and reason like humans, making it especially useful in fields requiring high interpretability and precision.

A SYMBOLIC AI EXAMPLE

In an unique project launched in 2019, The British Museum in London employed Symbolic AI to decipher and interpret ancient inscriptions from artifacts that had long puzzled historians. The project, known as the "Rosetta Project," aimed to unlock the stories behind thousands of artifacts dating back thousands of years, including Mesopotamian cuneiform tablets and Egyptian hieroglyphs.

The challenge was immense: many of these languages had limited existing translations or were partially understood, making conventional decoding methods slow and arduous. Enter Symbolic AI, which the museum's research team programmed with these ancient languages' known symbols, rules, and grammar. The AI was then tasked with analyzing inscriptions and comparing them against its database to identify patterns, fill in gaps, and propose translations.

This application of Symbolic AI was revolutionary for historical research. For the first time, historians were able to quickly interpret previously indecipherable texts, shedding new light on ancient civilizations' daily life, governance, and culture. One of the project's highlights was the interpretation of a previously unreadable cuneiform tablet, which revealed a new understanding of ancient Mesopotamian medical practices.

TIME SERIES ANALYSIS

DEFINITION

Time Series Analysis is the study of data points collected or recorded at successive time intervals to forecast future trends or patterns.

TIME SERIES ANALYSIS EXPLAINED

Time Series Analysis is a statistical technique that dives into data collected over time to uncover underlying patterns, trends, and cyclic behaviors. This method analyzes data points recorded at regular intervals—minutes, days, or years—to predict future values based on historical patterns. It's a powerful tool for forecasting, helping industries from finance to environmental science anticipate future conditions. By identifying trends, seasonal variations, and other components of time series data, analysts can make informed decisions, plan strategies, and identify anomalies. Whether predicting stock market movements, weather forecasts, or consumer behavior, Time Series Analysis provides a road map by translating past data into future insights.

A TIME SERIES ANALYSIS EXAMPLE

Satellites play a pivotal role in everything from global communication to national defense. For the United States Air Force, ensuring the operational integrity of these assets is not just a matter of technological pride but a critical national security imperative. Enter Time Series Analysis, which became a game-changer for the Air Force's satellite maintenance strategy.

In 2017, the Air Force's Space Command initiated a project to leverage Time Series Analysis to predict potential failures in satellite components before they occur. By meticulously analyzing historical data collected from satellites over the years—encompassing everything from orbital position changes and temperature fluctuations to on-board system behaviors—they developed models capable of foreseeing malfunctions.

This predictive approach allowed for preemptive maintenance and adjustments, drastically reducing the risk of in-orbit failures. One notable success story involved the early detection of a cooling system anomaly in a critical surveillance satellite. The model predicted a potential failure months before traditional monitoring methods would have flagged it. It enabled engineers to plan and execute a corrective maneuver that extended the satellite's operational life by several years.

TRANSFER LEARNING

DEFINITION

Transfer Learning is a technique in machine learning where a model developed for one task is reused as the starting point for a model on a second task, enhancing learning efficiency and performance.

TRANSFER LEARNING EXPLAINED

Transfer Learning is like giving a new student some textbooks from a course they still need to take, where the books are filled with notes and highlights from a previous student. This head start means they can learn some things from scratch.

In machine learning, this process involves taking a model trained on a large dataset for one task and re-purposing it for a different but related task. This is particularly useful when the new task has limited data available for training. Transfer Learning accelerates the training process, reduces the computational resources required, and often results in better models as they leverage previously learned patterns and knowledge.

A TRANSFER LEARNING EXAMPLE

In a innovative initiative, conservationists at Wildlife Protection Solutions, a global nonprofit, leveraged Transfer Learning to fight against poaching in 2019. Faced with the daunting task of monitoring vast, remote wildlife reserves, they turned to AI for a solution. The organization initially adapted a model for recognizing faces in social media photographs to identify individual animals and suspicious human activities in real time through drone and camera trap footage.

This AI system, named "Guardian," was trained on millions of images, learning to distinguish between species and individuals and even detect poachers' presence based on their behavior patterns. By reusing a model trained on human faces, the system could rapidly adapt to the nuances of wildlife monitoring with minimal additional training data, a critical advantage in areas where collecting extensive footage of rare animals or poachers is challenging.

"Guardian" transformed the fight against poaching. In its first year, the system significantly reduced poaching incidents in the reserves where it was deployed, proving that technology developed for one purpose could be transformed to serve another. This could potentially save thousands of lives across species.

TURING TEST

DEFINITION

A test of a machine's ability to exhibit intelligent behavior equivalent to or indistinguishable from human behavior.

TURING TEST EXPLAINED

The Turing Test, proposed by Alan Turing in 1950, is a benchmark for determining whether a computer can think like a human. The idea is simple: if a human interacting with an AI cannot reliably tell the machine apart from a human, the AI is considered to have passed the test. This test has sparked decades of debate and research into the capabilities and future of AI, pushing the boundaries of how we define intelligence. The British mathematician and computer scientist devised this test that challenges machines to mimic human responses and does so convincingly enough that a person cannot reliably tell the difference. It's not about the machine's knowledge or accuracy but its capacity for human-like conversation, encompassing wit, ambiguity, and nuance. The Turing Test has become a fundamental concept in the philosophy of artificial intelligence, sparking debates about what it means to "think" and whether a machine can possess genuine intelligence or consciousness.

A TURING TEST EXAMPLE

Although no AI has definitively passed the Turing Test by contemporary standards, various experiments have showcased the evolving capabilities of AI in mimicking human conversation. In 2014, at the Royal Society in London, one notable instance took place. A computer program named Eugene Goostman, simulating a 13-year-old Ukrainian boy, became the first to pass the Turing Test, albeit not 100%. Developed by a team of programmers led by Russian computer scientist Vladimir Veselov and Ukrainian Eugene Demchenko, Eugene fooled 33% of the human judges into believing it was human during a series of five-minute text-based chats.

Eugene's success sparked worldwide discussion about the future of AI and its potential impacts on society. Critics and supporters debated whether Eugene's ability to deceive judges truly signified intelligence or the skillful parroting of human conversation. The event underscored the evolving capabilities of AI systems in mimicking human-like responses, raising profound questions about what it means to be intelligent and whether machines might

Chapter Ten

FROM U TO Z

UNSUPERVISED LEARNING

DEFINITION

Unsupervised Learning is a type of machine learning where algorithms learn patterns from untagged data without explicit instructions on what to look for.

UNSUPERVISED LEARNING EXPLAINED

Imagine sorting a mixed collection of coins without knowing the denominations in advance. You might start by grouping them based on size, color, or engravings. Unsupervised learning works similarly; the algorithm analyzes data and tries to find natural groupings or patterns. This method helps discover hidden structures in data, like customer segments in marketing analyses or new trends in social media behavior.

UNSUPERVISED LEARNING EXAMPLE

In 2019, astronomers at the European Space Agency (ESA) embarked on an ambitious project using data from the Gaia space observatory, mapping the stars of our galaxy in unprecedented detail. With billions of data points on star positions, movements, and luminosities, the sheer volume of information was both a treasure trove and a challenge. Traditional analysis methods could not fully exploit this vast dataset, prompting the team to turn to Unsupervised Learning for help.

The AI algorithms deployed on Gaia's data were not instructed on what specific features to look for; instead, they were tasked with independently finding patterns or anomalies in the data. This exploratory approach led to the discovery of new stellar clusters and streams—groups of stars moving across the galaxy, remnants of smaller galaxies, and star clusters torn apart by the Milky Way's gravity.

This breakthrough provided valuable insights into the Milky Way's structure and history, revealing the dynamic processes shaping our galaxy. It showcased the power of Unsupervised Learning to uncover hidden patterns in complex datasets, opening new frontiers in the quest to understand the cosmos.

VIRTUAL REALITY (VR)

DEFINITION

Virtual Reality (VR) is a computer-generated environment with scenes and objects that appear real, making the user feel immersed in their surroundings.

VIRTUAL REALITY EXPLAINED

Virtual Reality is akin to stepping into a book or film, but you live within it instead of watching a story unfold. This technology uses headsets, gloves, and sometimes even full-body suits to simulate a user's presence in a digitally created space. Users can look around, move, and interact with the environment or objects within this space as if they were truly there. VR's power lies in its ability to create wholly controlled environments, from realistic simulations of the natural world to fantastical landscapes. This immersive experience is used for entertainment, education, training, and more, offering a new way to experience and interact with digital content.

A VIRTUAL REALITY EXAMPLE

In 2017, a trial in Germany leveraged Virtual Reality to revisit a crime scene from a different angle—quite literally. The case involved a complex reconstruction of a 1991 crime scene, where VR technology was employed to transport the courtroom into the past. Prosecutors used VR headsets to give jurors a 360-degree virtual walk-through of the crime scene, allowing them to understand the spatial dynamics and evidence placement in unprecedented detail.

This innovative approach marked one of the first times VR technology was used in a legal setting to enhance the jury's understanding of a crime scene. The use of VR helped jurors visualize the sequence of events as they happened, offering a more intuitive and immersive way to examine the facts of the case.

WEAK AI

DEFINITION

Weak AI, also known as Narrow AI, is designed to perform specific tasks without possessing consciousness, emotion, or self-awareness. Unlike strong AI, which exhibits generalized human cognitive abilities, weak AI operates within a limited pre-defined range or set of contexts.

WEAK AI EXPLAINED

Weak AI operates under a narrow set of conditions and parameters, excelling at specific tasks by following predefined rules and learning from data. Unlike its counterpart, Strong AI, which aims to replicate human cognitive abilities, Weak AI does not understand or interpret tasks in a human-like manner. Instead, it simulates human behavior based on algorithms and data processing. This form of AI is prevalent daily, from voice assistants on our phones to recommendation systems on streaming services. Its strength lies not in mimicking human thought but in efficiently handling tasks that would be time-consuming or impossible for humans to perform at the same speed and scale.

A WEAK AI EXAMPLE

In 2020, scientists from Pennsylvania State University and the University of California, Santa Cruz, embarked on an innovative project to predict volcanic eruptions using Weak AI. Focusing on the Fuego Volcano in Guatemala, one of the world's most active volcanoes, the team developed an AI system capable of analyzing seismic data to predict eruptions hours in advance.

This AI model, trained on years of seismic data from Fuego and other similar volcanoes, learned to identify the subtle patterns that precede an eruption. Unlike traditional monitoring methods, which require constant human observation and interpretation, this AI system provides continuous, automated surveillance of the volcano's seismic activity. In June 2020, the system successfully predicted an eruption several hours before it occurred, allowing for timely evacuations and significantly reducing the risk to nearby communities.

ZERO-SHOT LEARNING

DEFINITION

Zero-shot learning is a machine learning technique that enables models to recognize objects or concepts they haven't seen during training using descriptions or attributes.

ZERO-SHOT LEARNING EXPLAINED

Zero-shot learning pushes the boundaries of AI's capabilities by teaching machines to understand and classify information they haven't explicitly encountered before. Traditional machine learning models require extensive data on each category they're expected to recognize. In contrast, Zero-Shot Learning leverages an understanding of categories through attributes or relations described in the data it has seen, allowing it to make educated guesses about new, unseen categories. This approach is like teaching someone about animals they've never seen by comparing them to known animals with similar characteristics. It's particularly valuable when gathering training data is difficult or impossible, making AI systems more versatile and adaptable.

A ZERO-SHOT LEARNING EXAMPLE

In a project led by the Oceanographic Institute of Monaco in 2021, scientists applied Zero-Shot Learning to identify and catalog previously unknown species of deep-sea creatures. The deep ocean is Earth's final frontier, teeming with life that often evades detection and classification due to the sheer difficulty of accessing these extreme environments.

The team developed an AI model capable of recognizing and classifying deep-sea organisms based on their physical attributes and genetic information despite never encountering these species during its training phase. By inputting descriptions and known attributes of marine life, the model could predict the characteristics and potential classifications of new species captured in underwater camera traps.

This AI tool revolutionized marine biology, enabling researchers to identify and understand deep-sea ecosystems' biodiversity rapidly. For instance, it facilitated the discovery of a new species of bio-luminescent jellyfish, which the AI system linked to known species through shared characteristics, providing immediate insights into its behavior and ecology.

CONCLUSION

As we reach the end of "51 Essential AI Terms Explained for Leaders: A Non-Technical Guide," we must pause and reflect on the profound implications these terms, explanations, and insights can carry for you.

This book was crafted not just as a repository of definitions but as a bridge linking the intricate world of AI with the strategic imperatives of leadership. Through demystifying complex AI concepts and presenting them alongside tangible, real-world examples, we aimed to transform what might have appeared as an arcane science into a straightforward, accessible toolset that enhances your leadership impact.

The essence of this transformation lies in the application of knowledge. The concepts detailed within these pages—ranging from Machine Learning to Neural Networks, from Natural Language Processing to Zero-Shot Learning—are not merely academic. They are practical instruments for strategic decision-making, offering new perspectives and solutions to contemporary challenges. By weaving these AI insights into your leadership fabric, you augment your toolkit and significantly bolster your organization's capability to gain competitive advantage with your application of AI.

AI, like cybersecurity, is not a peripheral concern to be delegated or overlooked. It is integral to every aspect of modern business, from operational efficiency and customer engagement to innovation and competitive strategy. Your fluency in AI concepts enables you to engage more deeply with your technical teams, foster a culture of innovation, and lead with an informed view of potential and risk. This knowledge empowers you to foresee emerging trends, adapt strategies accordingly, and ensure your organization remains resilient and forward-looking.

Moreover, your mastery of AI principles extends your influence beyond the confines of your organization. It brings into light the critical conversations on AI readiness and ethical considerations in your industry, contributing to a broader understanding and responsible deployment of AI technologies. In doing so, you catalyze positive change, driving the collective advancement of your sector and the wider society.

However, the field of AI is dynamic and constantly evolving in response to new technological advancements, ethical discussions, and societal demands. The foundational knowledge you've gained here is just the start. The journey towards AI fluency is continuous and requires perpetual curiosity, learning, and adaptation. Resources for ongoing development include AI research publications, technology news outlets, and professional forums, each providing fresh insights and opportunities for application.

There are other books on AI for Leaders that I will be publishing very soon, and this book will act very much as a companion to them. But it also stands on its own as both a compass and a springboard, designed to inspire you to confidently embrace AI's complexities and leverage these insights for transformative leadership. The transition from uncertainty to understanding, from passivity to proactive engagement, signifies a pivotal development in your leadership journey. By demystifying AI, you've expanded your intellectual horizons and positioned yourself and your organization at the forefront of the digital age.

Thank you for allowing me to share part of your AI journey. Armed with the insights and understanding gleaned from this book, your next steps will not only fortify your leadership but also contribute to shaping a future where AI serves as a force for positive transformation.

Marco Ryan

London, March 2024

"51 ESSENTIAL AI TERMS EXPLAINED FOR LEADERS" REVIEW PAGE

"If your actions inspire others to dream more, learn more, do more and become more, you are a leader."
~ John Quincy Adams

We hope that you have found the book useful. I suspect that there are many other leaders out there, who were like you used to be. Less experienced, needing answers, but not sure who or what to trust.

Most people do, in fact, judge a book by its cover (and its reviews). So here's my request to you as an amazing leader who I know is committed to helping others succeed.

Please help that leader by leaving this book a review.

It's remarkably hassle-free, it doesn't cost you anything, it will take about 60 seconds and your review really could help.

If you are **on audible** - hit the three dots in the top right of your device, click rate & review, then leave a few sentences about the book with a star rating.

If you are reading on **kindle, iPad or other tablet** - scroll to the bottom of the book, then swipe up and it will prompt a review for you.

If for some reason these are working for you, then go to Amazon and leave a review right **on the book's page**. Here's the link:

https://www.amazon.com/review/review-your-purchases/?asin=1917220006

If all fails, **scan this QR code**:

Thank you for doing that. It makes more of a difference to the next leader, who may be considering whether to get this

book, than you realize.

Right, let's get back to the main event. On with more of those essential AI terms, definitions and explanations.

Thank you so much

Marco Ryan
London, March 2024

ABOUT THE AUTHOR

M arco is a renowned expert in digital transformation, data management, Artificial Intelligence, and Cybersecurity.

With a comprehensive understanding of the evolving digital

landscape, gained through years of Operational experience Marco brings a wealth of experience and expertise to guide readers through the world of Artificial Intelligence, Cybersecurity and Digital Transformation.

As the Cyber Leader in Residence at Lancaster University Management School and a former Global Chief Digital Officer and Senior Vice President Digital for BP, Marco is committed to empowering readers with the knowledge and skills necessary to navigate the digital future.

He has extensive public speaking experience, including Ted talks, regularly delivering Keynotes at major conferences or for companies as part of workshops or off-sites.

Marco has authored other books in the leadership impact series. The first of these was "51 Essential Cyber Terms for Leaders" and can be found on Amazon:

https://www.amazon.com/ESSENTIAL-CYBER-TERMS-EXPLAINED-LEADERS/dp/B0CXFQPNCH

To discuss options for working with Marco, whether for group or individual coaching or to explore having him deliver a keynote address, please use the QR code or click the link to his website.

https://marcoryan.com

RESOURCES

Khan, W., Ahmed, A. A. A., Vadlamudi, S., Paruchuri, H., & Ganapathy, A. (2021a). MACHINE MODERATORS IN CONTENT MANAGEMENT SYSTEM DETAILS: ESSENTIALS FOR IOT ENTREPRENEURS. *In Academy of Entrepreneurship Journal (Vol. 27, Issue 3, pp. 1–3).* https://www.abacademies.org/articles/Machine-moderators-in-content-management-system-details-essentials-for-iot-entrepreneurs-1528-2686-27-3-538.pdf

Admin, & Admin. (2023, November 10). Preparing for radical disruption - Revenue Pulse (RP). *Revenue Pulse (RP) - Marketing and Sales Operations.* https://www.revenuepulse.com/blog/preparing-for-radical-disruption/

Alkhorshid, Y., Aryafar, K., Bauer, S., & Wanielik, G. (2016). Road Detection through Supervised Classification.

arXiv *(Cornell University)*. https://doi.org/10.48550/arxiv.1605.03150

Schizas, C. N. (2016). Cognitive computing for supporting eHealth. *Health and Technology,* 7(1), 11–12. https://doi.org/10.1007/s12553-016-0162-2

Rudiger, R. (2021, August 2). *Get Machine Learning CNN GIF.* Congrelate. https://www.congrelate.com/get-machine-learning-cnn-gif/

Pokhalekar, D. D. (2018). A Study on Artificial Neural network, an evolutionary technique in Data mining [Journal-article]. *INTERNATIONAL RESEARCH JOURNAL OF MULTIDISCIPLINARY STUDIES,* 4(Special Issue 8), 1–2. https://core.ac.uk/download/236002699.pdf

Shyamala, R., & Maruthi, R. (2018). Diagnosis and prognosis of breast cancer using multi classification algorithm. *International Journal on Recent and Innovation Trends in Computing and Communication,* 6(8), 24–28. https://doi.org/10.17762/ijritcc.v6i8.5171

Bondaug-Winn, N. (2023, August 4). *Understanding the impact of autonomous vehicles on insurance agencies.* HBW Leads. https://www.hbwleads.com/blog/understanding-the-impact-of-autonomous-vehicles-on-insurance-agencies/

Harrer, S., Shah, P., Antony, B. J., & Hu, J. (2019). Artificial intelligence for clinical trial design. *Trends in*

Pharmacological Sciences, 40(8), 577–591. https://doi.
org/10.1016/j.tips.2019.05.005

Santhiya, C., & Padmavathi, S. (2023). Perspective Chapter: A
View – Cloud-Edge Computing Technology. *In IntechOpen
eBooks.* https://doi.org/10.5772/intechopen.111454

Hennick, C. (2020, May 6). Edge computing is on the rise among
energy and utility companies. *Technology Solutions
That Drive Business.* https://biztechmagazine.com/
article/2019/11/edge-computing-rise-among-energy-
and-utility-companies

Admin. (2023b, August 19). *Keeping passengers informed and
connected.* The Stay Update. https://thestayupdate.
com/keeping-passengers-informed-and-connected/

TRUSTroke webinar on Federated Learning | Knowledge Transfer.
(n.d.). https://knowledgetransfer.web.cern.ch/event/
trustroke-webinar-federated-learning

Ambolis, D. (2023, May 17). Exploring the power of generative
AI and its relation with blockchain. *Blockchain Magazine.*
https://blockchainmagazine.net/exploring-the-power-
of-generative-ai-and-its-relation-with-blockchain/

Bin Mohamad, S., Mohamad & University Teknologi PETRONAS.
(2015). *Modelling for Temperature Non-Isothermal
Continuous Stirred Tank reactor using fuzzy logic* [Thesis].
https://core.ac.uk/download/544133811.pdf

Lu, W., Mei, N., Gao, F., & Gao, X. (2015). Blind image quality
assessment via semi-supervised learning and fuzzy

inference. *Applied Informatics, 2*(1). https://doi.org/10.1186/s40535-015-0010-x

Tardif, A. (2023, April 22). *Unveiling the power of Large Language Models (LLMs)* – Search.AI.Wiki. https://search.ai.wiki/unveiling-the-power-of-large-language-models-llms/

Sightbox. (2023, May 24). *Machine Learning (ML) - Sightbox.* https://sightbox.co/ai_dictionary/machine-learning-ml/

NFTs Beyond Art: Exploring the emerging applications and use cases. (n.d.). https://imaginusvr.com/tpost/rlbxmtzao1-nfts-beyond-art-exploring-the-emerging-a

Jennings, R. (2024, January 12). *Glossary of Artificial Intelligence | AI Glossary.* Ai Is a Tool. https://machinelabs.ai/ai-glossary/

How AI and ML are changing the Technology Landscape? – TechMobius. (n.d.). https://www.techmobius.com/blogs/how-ai-and-ml-are-changing-the-technology-landscape/

Kaleem, S., Sohail, A., Tariq, M. U., & Asim, M. (2023). An improved big data analytics architecture using federated learning for IoT-Enabled urban intelligent transportation systems. *Sustainability, 15*(21), 15333. https://doi.org/10.3390/su152115333

Machine Learning Terms | Complete Machine learning & AI Glossary. (n.d.). https://www.activeloop.ai/resources/glossary/

Hakia. (2023, July 14). *The role of Ontologies in Semantic Technologies: Modeling and knowledge Representation*

-. Hakia: Covering All Angles of Technology. https://www.hakia.com/the-role-of-ontologies-in-semantic-technologies-modeling-and-knowledge-representation/

McCoy, J. (2023b, May 12). *Quantum of Finance: Meaning in banking.* Trustable Tech. https://www.trustabletech.org/quantum-of-finance-meaning-in-banking/

Machine learning - AI Wiki - Artificial Intelligence, Machine Learning Wiki and Guide. (n.d.). https://aiwiki.ai/wiki/Machine_learning

dataArchitect.Ai. (n.d.). *DataArchitect.ai.* dataArchitect.ai. https://dataarchitect.ai/ai-data-architecture

Mahant, M., Choudhary, B., Kesharwani, A., & Rathore, K. S. (2012). A profound survey on swarm intelligence. *In International Journal of Advanced Computer Research* (No. 1; Vol. 2, Issue 3, pp. 31–32). http://accentsjournals.org/PaperDirectory/Journal/IJACR/2012/3/6.pdf

Chandra, R., *, Agani, N., *, & Prihastomo, Y., *. (2012). Self driving car: Artificial intelligence approach. *Jurnal TICOM,* Vol.1(No.1), 43–44. https://media.neliti.com/media/publications/93435-EN-self-driving-car-artificial-intelligence.pdf

Introduction to data augmentation. (n.d.). Google Developer Student Clubs. https://gdsc.community.dev/events/details/developer-student-clubs-higher-institute-of-computer-science-ariana-presents-introduction-to-data-augmentation/

Rajput, K. (2014, April 18). *Artificial Intelligence Introduction* [Slide show]. SlideShare. https://fr.slideshare.net/kaushlendrarajput/artificial-intelligence-33691945

Yazdi, M. (2024). Augmented reality (AR) and virtual reality (VR) in maintenance training. In *Springer series in reliability engineering* (pp. 169–183). https://doi.org/10.1007/978-3-031-53514-7_10

Ambolis, D. (2023b, May 17). Exploring the power of generative AI and its relation with blockchain. *Blockchain Magazine.* https://blockchainmagazine.net/exploring-the-power-of-generative-ai-and-its-relation-with-blockchain/

Akhtar, Z. (2023, July 10). Artificial intelligence tutorial for beginners - DatabaseTown. *DatabaseTown.* https://databasetown.com/artificial-intelligence-tutorial-for-beginners/

Ienca, M. (2017). *Intelligent technologies for the aging brain: opportunities and challenges*. https://doi.org/10.5451/unibas-007132850

Joseph. (2022, August 18). What's the Difference Between Deep Learning and Supervised Learning? - reason. town. *reason.town.* https://reason.town/deep-learning-supervised-learning/

Pollution forecasting using Time series and LSTM with MXnet. (2023, May 11). https://stdin.top/posts/lstm-mxnet/

Mahant, M., Choudhary, B., Kesharwani, A., & Rathore, K. S. (2012b). A profound survey on swarm intelligence. *In*

International Journal of Advanced Computer Research (No. 1; Vol. 2, Issue 3, pp. 31–32). http://accentsjournals. org/PaperDirectory/Journal/IJACR/2012/3/6.pdf

Recruitment, A. (2022, November 14). *AI: The Quest for Superintelligence | Alldus.* Alldus. https://alldus.com/ blog/ai-the-quest-for-superintelligence/

Joseph. (2022a, August 15). What is an Example of Unsupervised Machine Learning? - reason.town. *reason.town.* https:// reason.town/example-of-unsupervised-machine-learning/

Made in the USA
Middletown, DE
24 April 2024

53444741R00066